WHAT ABOUT? SERIES

THE NEW COVENANT

FROM A MESSIANIC JEWISH PERSPECTIVE

WHAT ABOUT? SERIES

THE
NEW COVENANT

FROM A MESSIANIC JEWISH PERSPECTIVE

FIRST FRUITS OF ZION

Copyright © 2024 D. Thomas Lancaster. All rights reserved.
Publication rights First Fruits of Zion, Inc.
Details: ffoz.org/copyright

Publisher grants permission to reference short quotations (less than 400 words) in reviews, magazines, newspapers, web sites, or other publications in accordance with the citation standards at ffoz.org/copyright. Requests for permission to reproduce more than 400 words can be made at ffoz.org/contact. First Fruits of Zion is a 501(c)(3) registered nonprofit educational organization.

First Edition: 2011
Second Edition: 2024

Printed in the United States of America

ISBN: 978-1-941534-02-1

Scriptural quotations are from The Holy Bible, English Standard Version, copyright © 2001 by Crossway Bibles, a division of Good News Publishers. Used by permission. All rights reserved.

Scripture quotations from the New American Standard Bible®, Copyright © 1960, 1962, 1963, 1968, 1971, 1972, 1973, 1975, 1977, 1995 by The Lockman Foundation. Used by permission (Lockman.org). The author substituted "Messiah" for "Christ" and "Yeshua" for "Jesus" with permission from The Lockman Foundation.

Cover image: Page from the New English Translation Bible. Used by permission.

Quantity discounts are available on bulk purchases of this book for educational, fundraising, or event purposes. Special versions or book excerpts to fit specific needs are available from First Fruits of Zion. For more information, contact ffoz.org/contact.

First Fruits of Zion

Israel / United States

PO Box 649, Marshfield, Missouri 65706-0649 USA

Phone: (417) 468-2741
Website: ffoz.org

Comments and questions: ffoz.org/contact

To Boaz Michael

וַיָּקֶם אֶת־הָעַמּוּד הַשְּׂמָאלִי

וַיִּקְרָא אֶת־שְׁמוֹ בֹּעַז

CONTENTS

Introduction: What About the New Covenant? 1

1. The Covenant Maker 5

2. The Brit Chadashah 23

3. The Inner Torah 35

4. Better Promises 51

5. From Glory to Glory 67

INTRODUCTION:

WHAT ABOUT THE NEW COVENANT?

> For the Law proclaimed at Mount Sinai is now old and pertains only to you Jews; but this is for all universally: a new covenant has now been given to us, not according to the Law of Moses. (Justin Martyr, *Dialogue with Trypho* 11.4)

The second-century Gentile Christian Justin Martyr thought he had the new covenant and the old covenant all figured out. He was eager to tell the Jewish scholar Trypho all about it. According to Justin Martyr's interpretation, the old covenant was the Jewish law given at Mount Sinai. The new covenant was a universal revelation of God's grace bestowed on all of humanity. The new covenant replaced the now-obsolete old covenant, putting Christians and Christianity into the center of God's economy in the place of the Jews. It's called replacement theology: The new covenant replaces the old covenant, and the new people of God (Christians) replace the old people of God (Jews).

Contrary to the assumptions of Justin Martyr, Messianic Judaism teaches the ongoing authority of the Torah of Moses, the first five books of the Bible, i.e., the Law. In other words, we believe that Jesus Christ—Yeshua of Nazareth—did not come to abolish the Law, as he himself explicitly declares, "Do not think that I have come to abolish the Law or the Prophets; I have not come to abolish them but to fulfill them. For truly, I say to you, until heaven and earth pass away, not an iota, not a dot, will pass from the Law until all is accomplished" (Matthew 5:17–18). To put it yet another way, Messianic Judaism teaches that the laws of the Old Testament still apply today and that the Jewish people are still the chosen people of God.

Granted, the laws of the Torah do not apply universally to every person at every time. The Torah contains laws incumbent only upon Jews, laws incumbent only upon priests, laws incumbent only upon kings, and laws incumbent only when the Temple is standing. Moreover, Gentile disciples of Yeshua are exempt from a great many of the Torah's requirements. But the broad principle remains. Contrary to popular theology, Jesus did not cancel the Law or replace Israel with the church.

I encountered this startling realization when I first began attending a Messianic Jewish congregation. That controversial premise made me ask the question, "What about the new covenant?" Doesn't the new covenant cancel the old covenant? Consider what the Epistle to the Hebrews says, "Christ has obtained a ministry that is as much more excellent than the old as the covenant he mediates is better, since it is enacted on better promises. For if that first covenant had been faultless, there would have been no occasion to look for a second ... In speaking of a new covenant, he makes the first one obsolete. And what is becoming obsolete and growing old is ready to vanish away" (Hebrews 8:6-7, 13). That sounds pretty conclusive. Sounds like the old covenant is obsolete and the new covenant has replaced it.

Here's the contradiction. The New Testament teaches that Yeshua institutes a new covenant, but Yeshua himself says he did not come to abolish the old. He says that not a single jot or tittle will pass from the Torah until heaven and earth pass away. On the one hand, he institutes a new covenant that makes the old covenant obsolete and replaces it; on the other hand, he says he does not cancel the old.

The purpose of this book is to attempt to reconcile this seeming contradiction. My goal is to answer the question: "If Christ has not abolished the Torah, what about the new covenant?" The selection of material comprising this booklet originally came together for First Fruits of Zion's audio study, "What About the New Covenant?" Chapter one is based on our Bible study course titled *HaYesod: The Foundation*. The subsequent four chapters are from a series of sermons I delivered on the book of Hebrews to Beth Immanuel Messianic Synagogue in Hudson, Wisconsin. Those teachings have now been collected and edited into a two-volume commentary titled *The Holy Epistle to the*

Hebrews: Sermons on a Messianic Jewish Approach, and the astute reader of both works will recognize the duplication.

Consequently, the work of preparing and editing my original teachings from Hebrews for the sake of inclusion in the new commentary gave me the opportunity to update and revise this booklet as well—hence the second edition. In general, I have corrected several errors, upgraded the writing, and clarified the arguments presented in the first edition. I'm grateful for this opportunity to better answer the question, "What about the new covenant?"

May the LORD bless the disciple who applies himself to learn about the new covenant and the One who seals it with his blood. May God write his word upon your heart.

D. Thomas Lancaster

CHAPTER ONE
THE COVENANT MAKER

As a kid growing up in the church, I often heard teachers say, "We are under the new covenant now. The old covenant is done away with."

What does it mean to be under the new covenant? What is the difference between the new covenant and the New Testament? How is the new covenant different from the old covenant?

Covenant-making is a foundational concept that must be grasped to understand the Bible. The stories of the Bible build on a series of covenants. Covenants are deeply embedded within the text and fabric of the Bible. The Bible could rightly be described as a book of covenants.

According to the Bible, God relates to his people through covenant relationships. This makes the Bible difficult for a modern person to understand. We are familiar with contracts but not covenants. We tend to just read over the Bible's stories about covenants and ignore them when they occur in the narrative. Worse yet, since we do not understand how covenants worked in the ancient Near East, we tend to insert our own ideas and interpretations into the Bible.

The only exception might be the Christian marriage bond—a type of covenantal relationship that retains similarities to ancient covenants. However, the modern culture's cavalier attitude toward divorce and remarriage diminishes the usefulness of marriage as an example of covenantal obligation. Perhaps if married couples better understood the binding nature of covenantal relationships, more marriages might be salvaged from the disaster of divorce.

God is a covenant-making God, and he interacts with his people primarily through the definitions and terms of the covenant relationships he has established with his people. Consequently, every believer should desire to understand what a covenant relationship is and how it functions so that we can more effectively thrive in that relationship with our maker.

THE MEANING OF THE TERM "COVENANT"

What is a covenant?

The Biblical Hebrew word *brit* (ברית) appears in our English translations of the Bible as "covenant." Bible dictionaries define it as "a treaty, an alliance of friendship." Between individuals, it might be better described as a pledge on an agreement. Between a monarch and his subjects, it might function like a governing constitution.

Simply put, the *brit* is an agreement between two parties who agree to certain terms and stipulations that define the relationship between those parties. Covenants are more binding than simple contracts. Unlike contracts, which might expire at a specific date, covenants are considered permanent. In the world of the Bible, breaking a covenant was a big taboo.

Covenant-making involves an element of holiness and divinity. In the ancient world, a covenant usually required a sacrifice, religious rituals, and an invocation of the gods (or God). The deities became the wardens over the covenant; the gods were supposed to ensure that both parties kept their end of the deal. The covenanting parties often agreed on a token or sign of their covenant that would serve as a reminder of their obligations to one another.

In the Bible, the parties entering into a covenant sealed the new relationship with a shared meal. For example, Isaac and Abimelech shared a meal after making a covenant: "So he made them a feast, and they ate and drank" (Genesis 26:30). Jacob and Laban also shared a meal after making their covenant: "Jacob offered a sacrifice in the hill country and called his kinsmen to eat bread. They ate bread and spent the night in the hill country" (Genesis 31:54). At Mount Sinai, Moses, Aaron, Aaron's sons, and seventy elders over the tribes of Israel climbed Mount Sinai and ate a meal in the presence of God immediately after entering into covenant with him: "They beheld God, and ate and drank" (Exodus 24:11).

In the ancient Near East, covenants might be made between individuals, between families, between tribes, between nations, between political leaders, and so forth. One common type of ancient covenant called a Suzerainty treaty, defined the relationship between a great king and a vassal state from which the king demanded loyalty in exchange for protection and other benefits. Scholars have demonstrated how the entire book of Deuteronomy reads like an ancient Suzerainty treaty. See *Unrolling the Scroll* to see how Deuteronomy is laid out and organized like a Suzerainty treaty.

In the Torah's version of the covenant relationship, God takes the role of the great king. Israel is his vassal.

MUTUALITY, FIDELITY, TERMS, AND CONDITIONS

A covenant always contains terms and conditions to be fulfilled by both parties. They spell out the obligations. Ancient covenants were supposed to be mutually beneficial for both parties. That means that both covenanting partners had something good to get out of the covenant. The glue of the ancient covenant was a deep sense of fidelity. Covenant partners regarded themselves as absolutely devoted to one another, duty-bound to fulfill the terms and conditions of the covenant as a matter of covenant faithfulness.

The same principles apply to God's covenants with his people. When God entered into a covenant, he always imposed terms and conditions. The covenant created a mutual relationship from which both parties benefited. In addition, every covenant God makes requires fidelity and faithfulness on the part of both parties. There are no free rides. God will be faithful to man, and man is expected to be faithful to God.

THE BIBLICAL COVENANTS

The Bible records a series of covenants. God made a covenant with Noah, his children, and all life on earth not long after they disembarked from the ark. The covenant with Noah holds all of humanity to a certain basic level of ethical conduct. For his end of the agreement, God promised not to bring worldwide extinction through a global flood again. He set the rainbow in the clouds to function as a sign of the covenant—a reminder of its terms, conditions, and promises.

God made a covenant with Abraham. Abraham's son Isaac inherited that covenant and its promises, and his son Jacob inherited it from him. The LORD made a covenant with the whole nation of Israel at Mount Sinai, a covenant Christians often refer to as the "old covenant." He made a covenant with the sons of Aaron, promising them the dynasty of the Aaronic priesthood and guaranteeing them a perpetual role as Levitical priests. The LORD made a covenant with David and his sons after him, and of course, there is the new covenant.

All through the Bible God relates to his people by means of covenant relationships. He is the Covenant Maker. The whole Bible seems to be organized on the story of these covenants, their terms, conditions, promises, and fulfillments. The primary tension of the Bible occurs when people fail to meet their covenant obligations to God. The main plot of the Bible involves the long wait for God to fulfill his covenant promises to Abraham, to David, and to all Israel.

Despite the central role that covenants play in the Bible, it seems as if most Christian Bible readers do not really understand them or their relationship to one another.

THE COVENANT WITH ABRAHAM

God made a covenant with Abraham (Genesis 12, 15, 17, 22). This covenant differs from the covenant that God made with Noah and his sons in that this was not a universal covenant. The LORD made the covenant with Noah, with human beings, and all living creatures on earth. He made his covenant with Abraham with only a single person: Abraham.

Notice that the covenant that God made with Abraham did not cancel the covenant the made with Noah. Instead, the two covenants are both valid. They are not mutually exclusive. Similarly, all of the subsequent biblical covenants build on the covenant with Abraham. The covenant God made with Abraham provides a foundation for the rest. It does not compete with the other covenants; rather, the rest of the covenants build on it.

When God makes a covenant, it comes with terms and conditions. God's end of the bargain involves the covenant promises. The initial promises God makes to Abraham provide a sense of these provisions:

> Go from your country and your kindred and your father's house to the land that I will show you. And I will make of you a great nation, and I will bless you and make your name great, so that you will be a blessing. I will bless those who

bless you, and him who dishonors you I will curse, and in you all the families of the earth shall be blessed. (Genesis 12:1-3)

Later in the chapter, he adds two specifications regarding Abraham's seed. "To your offspring I will give this land," that is, the land of Canaan (Genesis 12:7), and "In your offspring shall all the nations of the earth be blessed" (Genesis 22:18).

Taking it all together, the LORD made several promises to Abraham. The LORD will:

- Make of Abraham a great nation.
- Bless Abraham.
- Make Abraham's name great.
- Make Abraham a blessing to others.
- Bless the ones who will bless Abraham.
- Curse the ones who curse Abraham.
- Give the land of Canaan to Abraham's seed.
- Cause all the families of the earth to be blessed through Abraham's seed.

TERMS AND CONDITIONS

The promises are God's end of the deal, but what was Abraham's obligation to this covenant? What were the terms and conditions that Abraham had to fulfill in order to meet his covenant obligations?

A popular Protestant teaching holds that Abraham had no covenant obligations. According to this idea, the Abrahamic covenant consisted only of God's grace because God made promises to Abraham with no conditions or strings attached whatsoever. That's not exactly true. Even from the outset, the LORD laid out conditions on these promises. To begin with, for Abraham's part, he needed to leave his home in Ur and travel to the land that God was going to show him. So, in a sense, from the outset, the promises entailed specific conditions. Abraham had to act in faith to receive the benefits promised to him. Throughout the Abrahamic narratives, God frequently tests Abraham's faith, measuring him to see if he will prove himself faithful to the covenant. For example, in Genesis 22, God tested Abraham's covenant loyalty by asking him to sacrifice his son Isaac:

> By myself I have sworn, declares the LORD, *because* you have done this and have not withheld your son, your only son, I will surely bless you, and I will surely multiply your offspring as the stars of heaven and as the sand that is on the seashore. And your offspring shall possess the gate of his enemies, and in your offspring shall all the nations of the earth be blessed, *because* you have obeyed my voice. (Genesis 22:16-18, emphasis mine)

God passes the covenant on to Abraham's son Isaac, explaining that the covenant with Abraham was indeed contingent on Abraham's faithful obedience. The LORD tells Isaac that he inherits the covenant "*because* Abraham obeyed my voice and kept my charge, my commandments, my statutes, and my laws" (Genesis 26:5).

Abraham believed God. He responded with faith, and he demonstrated his with faithfulness. Biblical faith is never just abstract belief or mental assent. It always results in the believer doing the Word of God. "Be doers of the word, and not hearers only, deceiving yourselves" (James 1:22). "What good is it, my brothers, if someone says he has faith but does not have works? Can that faith save him?" (James 2:14). According to James, a faith that has no accompanying action is not biblical faith. He cites Abraham as an example:

> Was not Abraham our father justified by works when he offered up his son Isaac on the altar? You see that faith was active along with his works, and faith was completed by his works; and the Scripture was fulfilled that says, "Abraham believed God, and it was counted to him as righteousness"— and he was called a friend of God. You see that a person is justified by works and not by faith alone. (James 2:21-24)

Biblical faith involves action. Faith and faithfulness are two sides of the same coin. God establishes this principle of "faith in action" as the foundational pattern for the covenantal response to his promises.

SIGN OF THE COVENANT

The biblical covenants came with an associated sign. The sign of the covenant with Noah was the rainbow. The sign of the covenant with Abraham is circumcision. He told Abraham to circumcise himself, his sons, and all the children born into his household, including his slaves. According to Genesis 17:14, a boy born into Abraham's family who is not circumcised is in violation of the Abrahamic covenant.

The covenant with Abraham did not die with Abraham. His son Isaac inherited it and passed it on to his son Jacob. Jacob passed it on to all of his children, the children of Israel. Therefore, the covenant with Abraham is a covenant for all Israel, and it has no expiration date. It is an ongoing covenant. Paul points out that even though God made later covenants with Israel, a later covenant does not set aside an earlier covenant:

> Even with a man-made covenant, no one annuls it or adds to it once it has been ratified. Now the promises were made to Abraham and to his offspring. It does not say, "And to offsprings," referring to many, but referring to one, "And to your offspring," who is [Messiah]. This is what I mean: the law, which came 430 years afterward, does not annul a covenant previously ratified by God, so as to make the promise void. (Galatians 3:15-17)

In other words, with God, a later covenant does not displace an earlier covenant.

THE COVENANT AT SINAI

Four hundred years after the LORD made the covenant with Abraham, he began to fulfill his promises to Abraham by rescuing his descendants from Egypt. He brought them out of Egypt and led them to Mount Sinai. Exodus 19-24 tells the story of the covenant that the LORD offered to the nation of Israel at Mount Sinai.

The covenant promises are God's end of the deal, and the Torah spells out those promises in several places. Leviticus 24 and Deuteronomy 27-29 spell out the rewards God offered Israel for covenant faithfulness and the punishments he offered for covenant infidelity. If Israel obeyed the covenant, the LORD promised to set the Jewish people above all other nations in the land he promised to give to their forefathers. He promised agricultural bounty, peace, prosperity, and blessing. If they did not keep the covenant, he promised imprecations and curses that would result in exile from the land.

The Torah spells out Israel's obligations to the covenant in several places. For example, from the outset of the covenant at Sinai, the LORD said to the people of Israel:

> If you will indeed obey my voice and keep my covenant, you shall be my treasured possession among all peoples, for all the earth is mine; and you shall be to me a kingdom of priests and a holy nation. These are the words that you shall speak to the people of Israel. (Exodus 19:5-6)

Israel's obligation is to obey God and keep the terms of the covenant. What are the terms of the covenant at Sinai? They are the laws of the Torah. In Deuteronomy 28, God promises to bless Israel "if" they "diligently obey the LORD ... being careful to do all his commandments." Likewise, he promises to bring curses upon Israel "if" they "do not obey the LORD ... to observe to do all His commandments and His statutes." The important word is the word "if." The contingency is obedience.

Faith was also a part of the equation. The first of the Ten Commandments is the commandment to believe in God: "I am the LORD your God, who brought you out of the land of Egypt, out of the house of slavery" (Exodus 20:2). Like the covenant with Abraham, the covenant at Sinai called for both faith and faithfulness.

THE SABBATH

The LORD designated the Sabbath as a sign for the covenant at Sinai. Unlike previous covenantal signs such as Noah's rainbow or Abraham's circumcision, the seventh-day Sabbath rest is not a physical object that takes up space in the physical universe. Instead, the Sabbath takes up time. It is an island of time. In his book *The Sabbath: A Sanctuary in Time*, Abraham Joshua Heschel teaches that, just as there are holy places, like the Temple, the Sabbath represents a holy place in time.

God instituted the Sabbath at the creation of the world. After the six days of creating, God rested—the first Sabbath. At Mount Sinai, he made the keeping of the Sabbath obligatory for Israel, and he established it as a perpetual sign of his covenant with Israel:

> The people of Israel shall keep the Sabbath, observing the Sabbath throughout their generations, as a covenant forever. It is a sign forever between me and the people of Israel that in six days the LORD made heaven and earth, and on the seventh day he rested and was refreshed. (Exodus 31:16–17)

A PERPETUAL COVENANT

Notice that the Torah says that the covenant at Sinai, marked by the keeping of the Sabbath, is a perpetual covenant. That's what the Bible says. God makes the Sabbath a sign of that covenant forever. How long does forever usually last? It's a long time. This means that God does not intend for the covenant he made at Sinai to expire—not so long as this world endures. Like the Abrahamic covenant, the Sinai covenant is ongoing. In fact, he made this covenant with the children of Israel as part of the fulfillment of the Abrahamic covenant.

Consequently, these covenants do not conflict with each other; they work together and build on top of one another. God made promises in the covenant with Abraham, and he began to fulfill those promises with the covenant at Sinai. The two covenants are not in competition with each other, they are closely related, one built on the other.

Breaking the covenant they made at Mount Sinai—for example, when Israel broke the covenant by making the golden calf—brought punishment, but it did not remove the Jewish people from their status as God's chosen nation. The covenant at Sinai came later than the Abrahamic covenant. When the covenant at Sinai failed (and it often did because the people failed to walk in obedience), the people fell back on the covenant promises that the LORD had made to Abraham. This happens over and over again in the pages of the Bible. After the sin of the golden calf, Moses reminded God of his covenant with Abraham, Isaac, and Jacob. On the basis of that earlier covenant, the LORD had mercy on the people. He spared the nation and renewed his covenant with them on the strength of the earlier covenant.

The Torah tells us that this is how the Sinai covenant is supposed to work. When the Sinai covenant is breached, God will still redeem his people and keep his covenant with them on the basis of the covenant he made with Abraham: "I will remember my covenant with Jacob, and I will remember my covenant with Isaac and my covenant with Abraham" (Leviticus 26:42).

The LORD's covenant with Israel did not begin at Sinai; it began with Abraham. "Is the law then contrary to the promises of God? Certainly not!" (Galatians 3:21). In other words, Paul asks, "Is the Torah opposed to the Abrahamic covenant?" Absolutely not. Both covenants are entirely complementary to one another, and the covenant with Abraham provides the basis for the covenant at Sinai.

THE COVENANT WITH AARON

The LORD made a covenant with Aaron, the brother of Moses, regarding the priesthood. "It is a covenant of salt forever before the LORD for you and for your offspring with you" (Numbers 18:19). In the ancient Near East, salt was used primarily as a preservative. A "covenant of salt" implies an enduring covenant. The covenant with the house of Aaron promises a perpetual right to occupy the Levitical priesthood: "Behold, I give to him my covenant of peace, and it shall be to him and to his descendants after him the covenant of a perpetual priesthood" (Numbers 25:12-13). That right of priesthood guaranteed provision from the altar and from the sacrifices, tithes, and offerings of the children of Israel, and it guaranteed an enduring dynastic succession so that Aaron would never lack a man to occupy the position of priest.

The terms and the conditions incumbent upon the sons of Aaron are spelled out primarily in the laws of the book of Leviticus and Numbers. There are a lot of them. For example, take a look at some of the requirements and prohibitions in Leviticus 21. The priests had to live at a higher standard of holiness than the rest of the nation. When priests failed to uphold those standards, they were punished severely. Think of Eli's sons, Hophni and Phinehas. Their line was cut out of the house of Aaron as a consequence of their covenant infidelity.

The sign of the covenant with Aaron can probably be best understood as the priestly garments themselves. The Bible goes into great detail describing the priestly garments and explaining their function as symbols of the perpetual status of Aaron and his sons. "You shall gird Aaron and his sons with sashes and bind caps on them. And the priesthood shall be theirs by a statute forever. Thus you shall ordain Aaron and his sons" (Exodus 29:9).

It's important to note that the covenant with Aaron does not obviate the Sinai covenant with the nation of Israel or the earlier covenant that God made with Abraham, Isaac, and Jacob. Instead, the new covenant with Aaron and his sons built on those previous covenants and assumed their ongoing validity.

THE COVENANT WITH DAVID

The LORD made a covenant with David and his descendants. Like the covenant with Aaron, the covenant with David is described as a covenant of salt: "The LORD God of Israel gave the kingship over Israel forever to David and his sons by a covenant of salt (2 Chronicles 13:5). The covenant promises to David are spelled out in an important messianic prophecy that God delivered to King David through the Prophet Nathan:

> I will make for you a great name, like the name of the great ones of the earth. And I will appoint a place for my people Israel and will plant them, so that they may dwell in their own place and be disturbed no more. And violent men shall afflict them no more, as formerly, from the time that I appointed judges over my people Israel. And I will give you rest from all your enemies. Moreover, the LORD declares to you that the LORD will make you a house. When your days are fulfilled and you lie down with your fathers, I will raise up your offspring after you, who shall come from your body, and I will establish his kingdom. He shall build a house for my name, and I will establish the throne of his kingdom forever. I will be to him a father, and he shall be to me a son. When he commits iniquity, I will discipline him with the rod of men, with the stripes of the sons of men, but my steadfast love will not depart from him, as I took it from Saul, whom I put away from before you. And your house and your kingdom shall be made sure forever before me. Your throne shall be established forever. (2 Samuel 7:9-16)

We can sum up the covenant promises, God's end of the deal, with two words: kingdom and dynasty. The LORD promised David posterity, inheritance, peace, greatness, and blessing—all the same things that he had promised to Abraham. The striking similarities between the promises to Abraham and the promises to David should indicate to us that the covenant with David is a further outworking of the covenant God made with Abraham. Like the covenant at Sinai, the covenant with David was built on the foundation of the Abrahamic covenant. It did not cancel or supersede the Abrahamic covenant or the Sinai covenant. Instead, it continued to work out the promises that the LORD originally made to Abraham.

The covenant that God gave to the house of David had terms and conditions. The LORD made the covenant contingent upon the obedience of the Davidic king. The LORD said that if the Davidic king "commits iniquity, I will discipline him with the rod of men, with the stripes of the sons of men, but my steadfast love will not depart from him" (2 Samuel 7:14–15). This means that God will not remove his covenant devotion. He will not break or cancel the covenant, but he will punish the disobedience of the Davidic kings. So long as David's sons walk in obedience, God will bless Israel with the peace, prosperity, and success promised in the covenant, but when the king commits iniquity, he invites chastisement and punishment on the nation. (According to these covenant obligations, all we need to bring the eternal kingdom is a sinless Son of David to rule over Jerusalem, a Son of David of whom the LORD will say, "I will be to him a father, and he shall be to me a son." This is, of course, the hope for the Messiah.)

What is the sign of the Davidic covenant? It's not a rainbow; it's not circumcision, and it's not the Sabbath. Instead, the LORD made "the house" into a sign of his covenant with David. This one involves some word play. David wanted to build a *house* for God, but God responded by saying that he would build a *house* for David, meaning his enduring dynasty. David's son Solomon would be the one to build the house of the LORD.

During the period of the First Temple, a qualified descendant of David ruled in Jerusalem. When Messiah—the true heir to David's throne—returns, he will rebuild the Temple, the sign of God's covenant with David.

The Davidic covenant demonstrates clear biblical continuity with the rest of Scripture. The covenant promises that the LORD gave to David brought further clarification and fulfillment of the covenant promises made to Abraham. To be specific, both Abraham and David were promised 1) a great name, 2) a piece of real estate, 3) offspring,

4) a connection to a throne, 5) an exclusive relationship with God, 6) an effect upon the nations, and 7) great blessing. In addition to having a connection to what has gone before, the Davidic covenant, like the Abrahamic covenant, laid the groundwork for the revelation of the Messiah.

After reviewing the covenant with Noah, the covenant with Abraham, the covenant at Sinai, and the covenant with David, we note that none of these covenants canceled previous covenants. Instead, they each built on the earlier covenants. At no point did the LORD say, "Forget about what I said before. Let's start all over with a brand new covenant." Each of the new covenants included and expanded on earlier covenants. Consequently, when we go to look at the new covenant, we should expect to find the same pattern.

NEW COVENANT

We might assume that we will find the information about the new covenant in the New Testament because the terms "new covenant" and "New Testament" mean the same thing. The New Testament is the new covenant, right? Wrong.

The New Testament is not the new covenant. The New Testament is a collection of writings that tell about how Yeshua initiates a new covenant, but the New Testament is not actually the new covenant itself. I would argue that the books of the New Testament should not be called the New Testament. They are "new" in that they are not as old as the Hebrew Scriptures. They are a "testament" in that they testify about Yeshua, but they are not the actual new covenant. They include the Gospels, a collection of four teaching biographies about Yeshua written by his apostles. They include the historical book called the Acts of the Apostles. They include the epistles written by the apostles and, finally, the Revelation, an apocalypse witnessed and recorded by the Apostle John. A better title for this collection might be Apostolic Scriptures. When we refer to them as the New Testament or New Covenant Scriptures, our theology tends to get twisted up.

So, where do we find the new covenant in the Bible? Prophecies about a new covenant—a future, Messianic-age covenant where God will redeem Israel and bring them back to their land—can be found throughout the books of the Prophets, particularly in Isaiah, Jeremiah, and Ezekiel. Subsequent chapters in this book will take a look at a few of those passages. The two key passages appear in Jeremiah 31 and Ezekiel 36. For now, here's a quick introduction to both:

> Behold, the days are coming, declares the LORD, when I will make a new covenant with the house of Israel and the house of Judah, not like the covenant that I made with their fathers on the day when I took them by the hand to bring them out of the land of Egypt, my covenant that they broke, though I was their husband, declares the LORD. But this is the covenant that I will make with the house of Israel after those days, declares the LORD: I will put my law within them, and I will write it on their hearts. And I will be their God, and they shall be my people. And no longer shall each one teach his neighbor and each his brother, saying, 'Know the LORD,' for they shall all know me, from the least of them to the greatest, declares the LORD. For I will forgive their iniquity, and I will remember their sin no more. (Jeremiah 31:31–34)

> I will take you from the nations and gather you from all the countries and bring you into your own land. I will sprinkle clean water on you, and you shall be clean from all your uncleannesses, and from all your idols I will cleanse you. And I will give you a new heart, and a new spirit I will put within you. And I will remove the heart of stone from your flesh and give you a heart of flesh. And I will put my Spirit within you, and cause you to walk in my statutes and be careful to obey my rules. You shall dwell in the land that I gave to your fathers, and you shall be my people, and I will be your God. (Ezekiel 36:24–28)

PROMISES AND TERMS OF THE NEW COVENANT

What are the promises of the new covenant? If I were to ask an Evangelical Christian, he might reply, "If you believe in Jesus, your sins will be forgiven, and you will go to heaven when you die." If I were to ask a Christian from the Roman or Orthodox confession, he might reply, "The promise that Christ has redeemed the church." According to what we read in the two preceding prophecies, however, the new covenant is a bit more involved with Israel and the Jewish people than it is with the individual sinner or the fate of the church.

In the new covenant:

- The LORD will write his Torah on his people's hearts (Jeremiah 31:33).
- The LORD will be their God (Jeremiah 31:33).
- Israel and Judah shall be God's people (Jeremiah 31:33).
- They shall all know the LORD (Jeremiah 31:34).
- The LORD will forgive their sin (Jeremiah 31:34).
- The LORD will regather the people of Israel to their land (Ezekiel 36:24).
- The LORD will spiritually cleanse Israel (Ezekiel 36:25).
- The LORD will give the nation a new heart (Ezekiel 36:26).
- The LORD will put his Spirit within them (Ezekiel 36:27).
- Israel will be faithful to the Torah (Ezekiel 36:27).

All of these, it turns out, are the promises and blessings of the previous covenants: the covenant with Abraham, the covenant at Sinai, the covenant with David, and even the covenant with Aaron. The new covenant fulfills all the promises of the previous covenants.

As with the other covenants, the new covenant demands faith and obedience. Faith because it says, "Everyone will know the LORD." Everyone will believe in God and have a relationship with him. Obedience because it says, "I will cause you to walk in My statutes, and you will be careful to observe My ordinances." It also says, "I will write my Torah on your hearts."

Unlike in the other covenants, however, the LORD guarantees the conditions of obedience by including them in the promises of the new covenant. God will do a mighty work in human hearts; he will personally guarantee Israel's end of the covenant by guaranteeing obedience, by changing hearts, by putting his Spirit within people, and by cleansing sinners. That's why he says that this covenant is not like the Sinai covenant. The new covenant is different, not because the LORD no longer requires obedience to the terms and conditions of his previous covenants but because the human beings trying to keep those terms and conditions will be changed.

THE COVENANTAL SIGN

The new covenant incorporates all the previous covenants and assumes the continuing validity of all the previous covenantal signs. Moreover, the new covenant seems to incorporate each of those signs for some further spiritual significance. Just as circumcision signified the Abrahamic covenant, the new covenant calls for a circumcised heart. Just as the Sabbath signified the covenant at Sinai, the new covenant offers the Sabbath rest of creation: the Messianic Era and the World to Come. The new covenant seems to incorporate the priestly garments signifying the covenant with Aaron in the resurrected bodies of the redeemed, clothed in white, and the resurrected body of the eternal high priest of the heavenly Temple. The "house" signified the covenant with David—both the "house" of David (i.e., the Davidic dynasty) and the house of the LORD (i.e., the Holy Temple). The new covenant creates a spiritual household of God, the temple of the Holy Spirit, hails the restoration of the Davidic dynasty in King Messiah, and promises the rebuilding of the Holy Temple in Jerusalem. In this way, the new covenant sweeps up and incorporates all the covenantal signs from the previous covenants without replacing the originals or rendering them obsolete.

In addition, the new covenant does come with its own unique signs. First and foremost is the resurrection of the Messiah, a token of the future fulfillment of the promises. On top of that is the endowment of the Holy Spirit. The apostles explain that God has "put his seal on us and given us his Spirit in our hearts as a guarantee" (2 Corinthians 1:22). God "has given us the Spirit as a guarantee" (2 Corinthians 5:5). The disciples are "sealed with the promised Holy Spirit, who is the guarantee of our inheritance until we acquire possession of it" (Ephesians 1:13-14). A guarantee is like a down payment, a security-pledge that guarantees that the rest of the payment will be made. In other words, we have not yet wholly entered the new covenant. The new covenant has not actually fully begun yet. We have not acquired possession of all its promises yet. We have only received the first installment on the whole of it.

That's obvious. Not everyone yet knows the LORD. The Torah is not yet written in full on our hearts. We still sin and break the commandments. Israel is not living in peace. Jerusalem has not been rebuilt as an eternal city, and so on and so forth. Many promises must be fulfilled before we can correctly say, "This is the new covenant." However, we can undoubtedly say that we have identified the Messiah who seals the new covenant with his blood and will deliver on its promises when he comes again. This is what he indicated, pointing toward the significance of his death and resurrection, when he took the cup at his seder and said, "This cup is the new covenant in my blood" (1 Corinthians 11:25).

God's covenants are eternal. Just as the covenant at Sinai did not cancel the covenant with Abraham, nor did the covenant with David cancel the covenant at Sinai or the covenant with Abraham, the new covenant does not cancel the previous covenants. Instead, it builds on them and improves on them.

GENTILES AND THE NEW COVENANT

One more thing about the new covenant: God did not make the new covenant with anyone other than the house of Israel and the house of Judah. He did not promise it to Gentiles. He did not make a new covenant with the Christian church. He promises to make a new covenant only with the Jewish people: "Behold, days are coming … when I will make a new covenant with the house of Israel and with the house of Judah." He makes the new covenant, just like all the other covenants, with his people Israel, the physical descendants of Abraham, Isaac, and Jacob.

That's great news for Jewish people, but it completely leaves Gentiles outside the new covenant—unless Gentiles can find a way to associate with Israel and participate with the Jewish people. The only Gentile covenant in the Bible is the covenant with Noah, and that covenant promises only that God will not end all life in a universal flood again. So how do Gentiles relate, in a covenantal sense, to God? If the new covenant is only for Israel, how do Gentile believers fit into it? Is there a covenant for them?

The answer is yes! Through allegiance to Messiah, the King of the Jews, the Gentile believer comes to benefit from the covenantal relationship that God made with his people Israel. Outside of relationship with Yeshua, Gentiles are "alienated from the commonwealth of Israel and strangers to the covenants of promise, having no hope and without God in the world" (Ephesians 2:12). As "strangers to the covenants of promise," they stand outside of the covenant with Abraham, the covenant at Sinai, the covenant with David, and the new covenant.

"But now in the Messiah Yeshua, you who once were far off have been brought near by the blood of the Messiah" (Ephesians 2:13). Notice that it does not say, "the covenant of promise," it says, "the covenants of promise." That is to say, all of the covenants.

This does not mean that Gentile believers become Jewish, and it certainly does not mean that the church replaces Israel as God's new covenant partner. It does mean that, through association with Yeshua, Gentile believers stand to benefit from the blessings and promises of the covenants, including the new covenant.

CHAPTER TWO

THE BRIT CHADASHAH

One of the first things I learned when I started attending a Messianic synagogue was that, contrary to everything the church had ever told me about the Law, Yeshua did not come to cancel the Torah. This discovery inspired me to wonder, "What about the new covenant?"

In Messianic Judaism, it's common to refer to the New Testament as the *Brit Chadashah* (ברית חדשה), i.e., the "new covenant." The Hebrew word *brit* means covenant, and *chadashah* is an adjective that means "new." Sometimes, Messianic apologists explain that the term *brit chadashah* actually means "renewed covenant." In other words, it's not a new covenant; it's the same covenant, renewed by Messiah. This explanation helps reconcile the contradiction I mentioned above, but it's not actually true. *Brit chadashah* does not mean "renewed covenant." It means "new covenant."

The modern Messianic Jewish movement did not create this euphemism. That literally is the way you would translate the words "New Testament" into Hebrew. It's the title that the church has assigned to the Greek scriptures left behind by the apostolic writers. Nevertheless, I'm not at all comfortable calling the New Testament the *Brit Chadashah* because the New Testament part of our Bible is not the new covenant.

OLD TESTAMENT, NEW TESTAMENT

Let me explain how replacement theology understands the difference between the two covenants. The Christian Bible contains two sections: an Old Testament (that is, the old covenant) and a New Testament (that is, the new covenant). The new covenant starts at Matthew 1:1. Everything that comes before the new covenant is part of the old covenant—part of the old deal that the new cancels. Theologically, this nomenclature has immense implications. It implies that the New Testament overrides the Old Testament, replaces it, and makes it obsolete. The new covenant, consisting of the canonical Greek Scriptures of Matthew through Revelation, cancels the old covenant, which consists of the canonical Hebrew Scriptures of Genesis through Malachi. That's how replacement theology understands the old and a new covenant, but it's wrong.

I used to volunteer for a local church as one of the teachers at a children's midweek Bible program. One night, I was supposed to teach the children the difference between the New Testament and the Old Testament. I asked them, "What do you think the difference is?" The five-year-old students did not know. The easiest way for me to explain the difference between the Old and the New, in a way that a five-year-old could grasp, was to say, "The Old Testament tells the story before Jesus was born. The New Testament tells about the time after Jesus was born. Before; after. Before; after."

Of course, there is more to it than that. The Old Testament consists of the canon of the Hebrew Scriptures; the New Testament consists of a collection of Greek writings attributed to the apostles, but I did not get into all of that with the five-year-olds. I tried to keep it simple: "Before Jesus; after Jesus."

AN OLD TESTAMENT CHRISTIAN

One of the primary leaders of the aforementioned children's program was also the mother of several of the children in the program. She homeschooled her children, took the work seriously, and had a lot of enthusiasm for children's education. She said to me, "I heard you keep the Sabbath on Saturday and do those Old Testament things."

"That's right," I admitted.

She seemed put off, as if I was judging her critically for not sharing my convictions. She retorted, "Well, I guess I'm a New-Testament Christian." By implication, that made me an Old-Testament Christian.

That was the end of the conversation, but here's the replacement theology underlying that brief exchange. Christians do not honor the Jewish Sabbath, the holy days, the dietary laws, and the other Jewish ceremonial laws of the Torah because those things applied only under the old covenant. They belonged to the old covenant. Back in the days before Jesus, human beings labored under the weight of the old covenant's impossible demands—under the Law. Now that Jesus has come and brought a new covenant, we are no longer under the old covenant. Under the new covenant, we no longer keep the old covenant rituals, which were only shadows of the reality in Christ.

HOW I LOST MY TEACHING JOB

One last story further illustrates the theology. I used to teach classes at a small, local seminary attached to a major metropolitan church. They hired me to teach a few Old Testament-type topics, and those classes were more-or-less well received. Then, they gave me the opportunity to teach a class titled "Introduction to the New Testament." I spent the first lecture explaining to the students that the New Testament is not the new covenant.

The difference between the old covenant and the new covenant is not the difference between the Old Testament and the New Testament. The old covenant is not the Old Testament; the new covenant is not the New Testament. The difference between the covenants is not the page in the Bible between the end of Malachi and the beginning of Matthew. We are still living in the old-covenant era. The new-covenant era is not yet here. The dean of the school terminated my employment for that lecture.

Like the directors of the seminary who dismissed me, you might be raising your own objections to such audacious statements. What do I mean by saying that the new covenant era has not yet begun? Didn't Jesus take the cup of the new covenant at his Last Supper? Doesn't Paul refer to himself and the other apostles as ministers of the new covenant? And doesn't the book of Hebrews refer to Messiah as the mediator of the new covenant?

NEW COVENANT IN JEREMIAH

To explain how the new covenant differs from the old, the Epistle to the Hebrews quotes a passage from the Prophet Jeremiah where the term "new covenant" first appears. The theology and significance of the new covenant is one of the central ideas in the Epistle to the Hebrews, so we need to understand it well before attempting to press much further into the epistle. This chapter focuses on identifying the new covenant.

The side-by-side chart below compares Hebrews 8:8-12 with the prophecy of the new covenant in Jeremiah 31:31-34.

Hebrews 8:8-12	Jeremiah 31:31-34
For he finds fault with them when he says: "Behold, the days are coming, declares the Lord, when I will establish a new covenant with the house of Israel and with the house of Judah, not like the covenant that I made with their fathers on the day when I took them by the hand to bring them out of the land of Egypt. For they did not continue in my covenant, and so I showed no concern for them, declares the Lord. For this is the covenant that I will make with the house of Israel after those days, declares the Lord: I will put my laws into their minds, and write them on their hearts, and I will be their God, and they shall be my people. And they shall not teach, each one his neighbor and each one his brother, saying, 'Know the Lord,' for they shall all know me, from the least of them to the greatest. For I will be merciful toward their iniquities, and I will remember their sins no more."	Behold, the days are coming, declares the LORD, when I will make a new covenant with the house of Israel and the house of Judah, not like the covenant that I made with their fathers on the day when I took them by the hand to bring them out of the land of Egypt, my covenant that they broke, though I was their husband, declares the LORD. But this is the covenant that I will make with the house of Israel after those days, declares the LORD: I will put my law within them, and I will write it on their hearts. And I will be their God, and they shall be my people. And no longer shall each one teach his neighbor and each his brother, saying, "Know the LORD," for they shall all know me, from the least of them to the greatest, declares the LORD. For I will forgive their iniquity, and I will remember their sin no more.

Some historical context helps to clarify the significance of Jeremiah's prophecy about the new covenant. The Prophet Jeremiah lived in a turbulent time in Jewish history, just before the Babylonian destruction of Jerusalem in 586 BCE. The LORD gave him an unpopular message to deliver to the people of Jerusalem: "You have broken God's covenant, and this city is going to fall to the Babylonians! This Temple will be destroyed with it, and the people will go into exile. Judgment is coming." That was Jeremiah's message. All of these terrible outcomes were destined to befall the nation because the people had violated God's covenant.

In the new covenant passage, Jeremiah shifts away from his prophet-of-doom mode and speaks of a time of future hope. He speaks of a new covenant that will be unlike the old covenant. Under the old covenant, the LORD punished his people for violating the terms of the covenant by sending them into exile. Under the new covenant, Jeremiah said, the LORD would forgive the sins of the nation. They would no longer need to suffer the punishments incurred by their sins.

Israel's history follows a cyclical pattern through the pages of the Bible. The people sin, stray from the Torah, and violate their covenant obligations. The LORD sends punishment in the form of natural disasters, foreign invaders, exile, or all of the above. The people cry out to the LORD. He raises up a redeemer for them. The redeemer rescues the people and establishes them in covenant fidelity. A generation elapses, and the cycle begins again as the people sin, stray from the Torah, and violate their covenant obligations. It's a theme that runs through the whole Bible. It's the pattern of exile and redemption.

Jeremiah utters the prophecy of the new covenant just as the nation of Judah is about to go into exile. The prophecy offers hope for a future redemption—not just another redemption in the endless cycle of exile and redemption, but a final redemption: the end of all exiles. To permanently redeem the people from exile so that the nation never needs to undergo such a punishment, the LORD needs to change the system—otherwise, he will get the same results. He could redeem Israel a thousand times, and each time, the sin of the nation would eventually incur another round of exile. To break the cycle, the LORD introduces the new covenant.

WHAT WAS THE OLD COVENANT?

A covenant is an agreement or treaty between two parties. It spells out terms and obligations incumbent on both parties. In this case, the terms and obligations incumbent on Israel are the laws of the Torah.

Jeremiah explains that the new covenant will not be like the old covenant the LORD made with Israel at Sinai (Jeremiah 31:32). When Israel first arrived at Mount Sinai, the LORD offered to take the people into a privileged covenant relationship. The offer came with one important contingency: "If you will indeed obey my voice," meaning, "If you will obey me" (Exodus 19:5-6). The people agreed to heed God's voice and obey whatever terms and conditions he might impose. They said, "All that the LORD has spoken we will do." Moses reported their reply to the LORD (Exodus 19:8). The voice from the mountain uttered ten commandments, and Moses received further terms and conditions to deliver to the people. Then Moses initiated them into a covenant by means of certain rituals and ceremonies described in Exodus 24:3-7. Moses recorded the terms and conditions in a document called the book of the covenant. The agreement consisted of the assent of the people, "All that the LORD has spoken we will do, and we will be obedient." The laws of the Torah are the terms and conditions of the covenant. However, the actual covenant is the agreement between God and Israel that defines the relationship and stipulates the rewards and punishments for fidelity to the covenant's terms.

The LORD offered the covenant to Israel, saying, "If you will indeed obey my voice and keep my covenant (which entails obedience to the laws of Torah), you shall be my treasured possession among all peoples … a kingdom of priests and a holy nation." The converse of this offer is, "If you disobey me and break my covenant (by disobedience to the laws of the Torah), then you will not be my people."

The Torah contains the terms and obligations of the covenant, but the laws of the Torah are not the covenant itself. The Torah tells the story of the covenant, and it presents its laws and instructions in covenantal form, but for purposes of understanding the difference between the old covenant and new covenant, we have to distinguish between the agreement and the terms and conditions agreed upon because the Prophet Jeremiah makes the same distinction when he introduces the new covenant.

BETTER COVENANT AND BETTER PROMISES

The writer of the book of Hebrews claims that the Messiah, in his role as heavenly high priest, meditates the new covenant. He has "obtained a ministry that is as much more excellent than the old as the covenant he mediates is better, since it is enacted on better promises" (Hebrews 8:6). The heavenly priesthood is superior to the priestly order of Aaron by a proportion of the same exponent as the excellency of the new covenant exceeds that of the old. The new covenant, after all, is based upon far better promises than the promises the old covenant contained. (We will take a subsequent chapter to explore those "better promises" in detail.) Under the terms of the new covenant, God need no-longer punish the nation for iniquities because he alters human nature to remove man's propensity to sin. The LORD says that the new covenant is "not like the covenant that I made with their fathers on the day when I took them by the hand to bring them out of the land of Egypt, my covenant that they broke" (Jeremiah 31:32).

The new covenant will not be predicated on the contingency, "If you obey my Torah," or on the terms, "All that the LORD has spoken we will do, and we will be obedient." In the new covenant, the LORD says, "I will put my law within them, and I will write it on their hearts" (Jeremiah 31:33). In the old covenant, God spoke his Torah, Moses wrote it in a book, and the people said, "Everything God has said, we will do." In the new covenant, God puts his Torah within his people and writes it on their hearts. This means that, in the new covenant, the laws of the Torah will not be external to a person as criteria he or she must meet, nor will it consist of rules to which he or she must submit as much as it will be written out within a person as part of his or her essential nature. This "Inner Torah" will be revealed in the Messianic Era as part of the revelation of the Torah of Messiah. The Inner Torah will not be a different Torah. God did not say, "I will put a new Torah within them, and I will write a new Torah on their hearts." It's the same Torah with the same standards and the same commandments "until heaven and earth pass away," but it will be internal to the person and not external (Matthew 5:18).

WHAT'S WRONG WITH THE OLD COVENANT?

The writer of the book of Hebrews indicates that the old covenant had a critical fault that required its dissolution and the formation of a new covenant:

> If that first covenant had been faultless, there would have been no occasion to look for a second. For he finds fault with them when he says: "Behold, the days are coming, declares the Lord, when I will establish a new covenant with the house of Israel and with the house of Judah." (Hebrews 8:7-8)

Was the Torah really faulty? The Scriptures unanimously concur, "The Torah of the LORD is perfect" (Psalm 19:8[7]). The Torah is perfect, but the imperfections of the nation limit the covenant agreement to keep the Torah. The fault in the old covenant was in the people who made the agreement. The people were at fault, not the Torah. The Epistle to the Hebrews explains, "*For he finds fault with them.*" Israel agreed, "Everything the LORD has said we will do," but they did not keep their end of the agreement. The writer of the Epistle to the Hebrews says, "For he finds fault with them when he says [in Jeremiah]: 'Behold, the days are coming, declares the Lord, when I will establish a new covenant with the house of Israel and with the house of Judah'" (Hebrews 8:8).

The problem with the old covenant was not that the Torah was too strict, too legalistic, too difficult, or anything like that at all. The fault with the old covenant did not lie in the laws of the Torah or its ceremonies; the fault lay with the people: "He finds fault with them when he says ... I will establish a new covenant."

To put it succinctly, the problem with the old agreement, which consists of obeying everything God has commanded, is sin. People are faulty. All have sinned and fallen short of the glory of God. Something had to change.

What should God do to rectify this problem? Should he lower the bar by altering the criteria of righteousness? Did the LORD say to the people of Judah, "I guess that Torah thing didn't work. Let's start over. Now, you can sin all you want. I'll change my Law so that it won't be so difficult"?

God does not change.

His Torah does not change.

Instead, he changes people.

He can do that because he made us. He can change us, and this is how he has chosen to make a new covenant. He will, through his Spirit, write his Law on human hearts. This is one of the better promises of the new covenant and a promise of the Messianic Era.

THE RENEWED COVENANT

The LORD says that the new covenant will not be like the covenant he made with Israel at Mount Sinai. This is why I don't like referring to the new covenant as the "renewed covenant." Renewed covenant implies the same covenant reinstated. If the new covenant is just a renewed version of the covenant at Sinai, it's really not that remarkable. Israel conducted covenant renewal ceremonies at several points in biblical history. They renewed the covenant in the days of Ezra and Nehemiah, in the days of King Josiah, in the days of King Hezekiah, in the days of the Prophet Samuel, and in the days of Joshua. They even renewed the covenant in the days of Moses. In fact, the LORD renewed the covenant with the nation just eighty days after Israel broke it the first time by making a golden calf. Moses interceded for Israel, and the LORD renewed the covenant. The renewed covenant had a new set of tablets to replace the ones Moses broke. Moses also renewed the covenant with the nation before they crossed the Jordan, and he gave them instructions to routinely renew the covenant with a public reading once every seven years.

If the new covenant is just a renewed version of the covenant at Sinai, it won't fare any better than it has before. On the contrary, the prophecy explicitly states this is not merely a "renewed" covenant. It will not be "like the covenant that I made with their fathers on the day when I took them by the hand to bring them out of the land of Egypt."

When Messianic teachers refer to the new covenant as a renewed covenant, they are attempting to correct the idea that the new covenant overturns and abolishes the Torah. That idea does need to be corrected. The new covenant is unlike the one God made with Israel at Sinai, but that does not mean that the new covenant has new laws and standards unlike the ones he gave Israel at Sinai. The laws and standards of righteousness have not changed. The Sabbath day has not changed to some other day. The prohibition against working on the Sabbath has not been relaxed. The prohibition against idolatry has not been altered. The new covenant has not canceled the dietary laws. The new covenant has not suspended the commandment to circumcise a Jewish boy on the eighth day. In regard to the laws, commandments, stipulations, and judgments of the Torah, the new covenant is exactly like the old covenant.

The difference is the people. The people are what change.

CONFUSION ABOUT GENTILES

It's easy to see how the thinking of theologians became confused over this. Early Gentile Christian teachers in the second and third centuries knew from the teaching of the apostles that they were not required to circumcise their sons or keep other ceremonial commandments of the Torah. They just didn't know why that was. As the Christian church began to adopt replacement theology and think of themselves as the true Israel, they had to explain why they, the true Israel, did not keep those specific laws that God gave to Israel.

To solve this riddle, they mistakenly assumed that a momentous change in the law must have taken place with the death of Jesus. (A momentous change did take place, but it wasn't the cancellation of the Torah's laws.) They conflated Paul's epistles with the discussion about the new covenant in Hebrews 8 and assumed that, since the new covenant had gone into effect, it must have canceled the Jewish ceremonial laws. That's how they understood it, and that's still taught in the churches today.

This mixed-up theology results in deep misunderstandings. For example, Jewish believers are routinely told that, under the new covenant, they no longer need to be Jewish or practice the Torah. They no longer need to keep the Sabbath, the holy days, the dietary laws, or any of the ceremonies of Judaism. The new covenant sets them free from their obligations to the Torah.

A clear-eyed reading of the New Testament reveals that the rules for the Jewish people have not changed, and neither have the rules for the Gentiles. The Torah distinguishes between Jews and Gentiles; Judaism distinguishes between Jews and Gentiles, and so did the apostles. Some of the Torah's laws apply to all people; some apply only to Jewish people. That's not new. That's not something that changed at the cross. God's righteous standards do not change. His definition of sin does not change. What needed to change, if the LORD was going to redeem his people, was the people.

It's a terrible oversimplification (and terribly wrong) to teach that a Gentile Christian is exempt from circumcising his son because the new covenant releases him from the obligation of circumcision. That's not the case at all. Even under the old covenant, the Gentile had no obligation to circumcise his son. That law pertained only to Jewish people. The apostles exempted Gentile disciples from the practice of circumcision because the Torah exempted Gentiles from circumcision. The distinction between Jews and Gentiles did not begin with the institution of the new covenant.

The new covenant does not change God's Torah. It changes God's people by forgiving their sins, removing their iniquity, and placing his Torah within them. In this way, the LORD will bring an end to the cycle of exile and redemption. As Paul says, "All Israel will be saved." The Jewish people will never go into exile again.

BINDING OF SATAN

In the coming kingdom, under the new covenant, people will be different than they are today. During the Messianic Era, the evil inclination within human beings will be subdued. This is what it means when the Apostle John says, "He seized the dragon, that ancient serpent, who is the devil and Satan, and bound him for a thousand years, and threw him into the pit, and shut it and sealed it over him, so that he might not deceive the nations any longer, until the thousand years were ended" (Revelation 20:2-3). People will be different. Not just forgiven, we will become new creations with new natures. When the Messianic Era comes, and the Torah of Messiah will be revealed, the Spirit will place that Torah within us, and we will be transformed.

This has not happened yet, at least not for me. It's clear to me that I am not a new-covenant Christian because my evil inclination is still alive, kicking, and, unfortunately, not yet fettered in chains.

The new covenant is the covenant for the kingdom, the covenant for the Messianic Era, and ultimately, the covenant for the resurrected in the World to Come, who will be sinless "like angels in heaven" (Mark 12:25). The new covenant has not yet arrived because the new era has not yet arrived. But it has begun to draw near. The gospel message declares that people should repent now because the kingdom is at hand. Our Master has initiated the new covenant already in his resurrection, and he beckons us to take hold of it and let the Spirit of God begin the process of placing his Torah within us and writing his Torah on our hearts.

Until the kingdom comes, it is the job of every disciple to strive to attain this new covenant of the Messianic Era now, in this world, and to bring that revelation of the Inner Torah home to bear now. We invite God's Spirit to write his Word on our hearts. We beseech him to put Satan in chains now by subduing our evil inclinations. Our objective is to live in the kingdom now, even though we are not there yet.

In order to do this, however, we need to acknowledge that the Inner Torah God writes on our hearts cannot be a different Torah from the one that Moses recorded. God is not changing his Law; he is changing our hearts. This realization has practical implications. It allows us to check our impulses against the written word of Scripture to confirm that it is indeed the Spirit of the LORD at work within us. It also means that, as the Torah is written on our hearts, we do well to conform our lives more closely to it. That process might sometimes result in a mode of worship and faith that others might characterize as "old covenant." You might find yourself labeled as an Old-Testament Christian, especially by those who identify themselves as New-Testament Christians. If that happens, just remember, it's the new covenant at work within you that makes you look "Old Testament" to others.

CHAPTER THREE
THE INNER TORAH

Once, I was teaching a Torah class as part of the adult education program in a large, charismatic church. One of my students, an Evangelical woman from another charismatic church, expressed a lot of excitement over what she was learning. After several weeks, she managed to persuade her husband to come to the class with her, but he did not share her enthusiasm for Torah study. He was a spiritual and godly man. I know he was a devout Christian, but he was clearly not happy with my teaching that night.

That particular night, I happened to be teaching about the relationship between the giving of the Torah at Shavu'ot and the giving of the Spirit at Pentecost. I also taught the passages from the prophets indicating that, in the Messianic Era, God will place his Spirit within us to enable us to walk in his statutes and keep his commandments.

After the class, the fellow merely remarked that all of this sounds like the "oldness of the letter and not the newness of the Spirit."

That was the last time I saw him or his wife. But I mused over the remark, wondering if, on the way home that night, the man and his wife might inadvertently drive through an intersection without coming to a complete stop at the stop sign. I imagine a police officer pulls them over. The man pleads innocence on the basis that the word STOP is merely the oldness of the letter of the law, whereas the newness of the Spirit indicates that, so long as he has his heart in the right place and he doesn't collide with another vehicle, he need not literally stop at stop signs.

THE SPIRIT AND THE LETTER

Have you ever heard anyone contrast the spirit of the Law against the letter of the Law? Usually, in Judaism, this type of language denotes the difference between a specific commandment and the intention of a commandment. For example, the specific mitzvah requires us to make a parapet around our roof. That is the letter of the law, but the spirit of the law requires us to remedy any dangerous hazard on our property to prevent accidents. That's the intention of the commandment.

Replacement theology uses the terminology to a different effect. From that perspective, the letter of the Law refers to the specific written commandment and the requirement to literally observe what the Bible says. In contrast, the spirit of the Law refers to a looser, less legalistic, less litigious interpretation of the law that allows for more flexibility—sort of a loophole from actual obedience to what the Bible says, which renders the commandments optional. For example, the letter of the law prohibits tattoos (Leviticus 19:28), but the spirit of the law permits tattoos because tattoos are cool.

So, the concept of the spirit versus the letter functions as a spiritual loophole to provide an out from heeding the commandments. It's slippery thinking. I have heard people justify leaving a spouse to be with someone else on the basis that the Spirit "released them" from the marriage.

The concept of spirit-versus-letter is derived from Paul's epistles:

> Circumcision is a matter of the heart, by the Spirit, not by the letter. (Romans 2:29)

> Now we are released from the law, having died to that which held us captive, so that we serve in the new way of the Spirit and not in the old way of the written code. (Romans 7:6)

> [He] has made us sufficient to be ministers of a new covenant, not of the letter but of the Spirit. For the letter kills, but the Spirit gives life. (2 Corinthians 3:6)

It's hard to argue with those words. It sounds like the letter of the Law (the literal written Torah) has been overturned by a more spiritual, internalized, subjective law. After all, in the new covenant, God writes his Law on your heart, not on tablets of stone. But before we slip too far down the slope of moral relativism, let's take a closer look at this dichotomy.

REVIEWING THE NEW COVENANT

In the previous chapter, I attempted to dispel some common misconceptions about the new covenant. "New covenant," the *brit chadashah*, does not mean "renewed covenant" as is often taught in Messianic Judaism. It means "new covenant." I demonstrated that the new covenant is not the New Testament. That's a misnomer. The distinction between new covenant and old covenant is not the same as the distinction between faith and deeds, nor is it the same as the distinction between grace and Torah.

Contrary to appearances, the old covenant is not the same as the laws of the Torah. Instead, the old covenant was Israel's agreement to keep the laws of the Torah. In the old covenant, the Torah was written on tablets of stone and as ink on parchment scrolls, but in the new covenant, the Torah will be placed within human beings, written on human hearts (Jeremiah 31:33). This indicates that the term "old covenant" is not just another term for the Torah because the Torah will also be a central part of the new covenant.

In the previous chapter, I also made the provocative statement that we have not yet entered the New Covenant Era. That should be obvious in that the new covenant includes a universal revelation of the LORD:

> No longer shall each one teach his neighbor and each his brother, saying, "Know the LORD," for they shall all know me, from the least of them to the greatest, declares the LORD. (Jeremiah 31:34)

Under the new covenant, every human being on earth will know the truth and have knowledge of the Almighty God. Currently, on planet earth, that is not the situation. We know that we have not yet entered this New Covenant Era because not everyone knows God.

Under the new covenant, God will forgive the iniquity of Israel and Judah and "remember their sin no more." The sins of the nation, from the golden calf all the way to the coming of the Messiah, will be pardoned and "remembered no more." Two thousand years of Jewish suffering indicates that we have not yet entered that moment of ultimate reconciliation.

FALSE DICHOTOMY

Replacement theology argues against the ongoing relevance and authority of the Torah on the basis of this very passage from Jeremiah. People say, "In the old covenant, we had to keep the Torah, but now that we are under the new covenant, the Torah is written on our hearts."

The sentiment is wrong on two counts. It's wrong to suppose that the Torah written on human hearts will in some way contradict the written Torah. For example, if the written Torah says, "Thou shalt not," the Torah written on human hearts cannot say, "Thou shalt." That's sloppy theology. God does not change, and his Torah does not change.

Neither is it correct to suppose that we have already arrived at that state where the Torah is within us and written on our hearts. Our sins betray the truth of the matter. If the Torah is written on my heart, it's written in invisible ink. Until then, it remains an aspirational goal for everyone, as Moses expressed it in the greatest commandment:

> You shall love the LORD your God with all your heart and with all your soul and with all your might. *And these words that I command you today shall be on your heart.* (Deuteronomy 6:5-6, emphasis mine)

We create a false dichotomy when we contrast the Torah of Moses against the Torah of the heart as if they were two different Torahs. They are the same Torah, but as we learned in the previous chapter, the difference is not the Torah; the difference is us. In the new covenant, God reprograms us, so to speak, by writing his Torah on our minds. Those who enter the kingdom will do so as new creations, internally rewired by the revelation of God. Ultimately, the new covenant needs to be understood as God's covenant with Israel for the Messianic Era. In the Messianic Era, things will be different. The evil inclination of human beings will be chained and imprisoned so that it cannot "deceive the nations any longer" until the thousand years are complete (Revelation 20:3).

THE SIGN OF THE NEW COVENANT

Every covenant in the Bible comes with a sign that functions as a token of the covenant. The covenant with Noah had the sign of the rainbow. The covenant with Abraham had the sign of circumcision. The covenant at Sinai had the sign of the Sabbath. The covenant with David had the sign of the "house": the dynasty of David and the Holy Temple.

What is the sign of the new covenant? The apostles indicate that the sign of the new covenant is the outpouring of the Holy Spirit. Paul says that God "has also put his seal on us and given us his Spirit in our hearts as a guarantee" (2 Corinthians 1:22). A few chapters later, he uses the same language again, stating that God has "given us the Spirit as a guarantee" (2 Corinthians 5:5). In the first chapter of Ephesians, he refers to the Holy Spirit as a promise for the Messianic Era and a guarantee of our inheritance:

> In him you also, when you heard the word of truth, the gospel of your salvation, and believed in him, were sealed *with the promised Holy Spirit, who is the guarantee of our inheritance* until we acquire possession of it, to the praise of his glory. (Ephesians 1:13–14, emphasis mine)

These statements indicate that the Holy Spirit works within the disciples as a deposit on the whole amount that remains to be paid at the resurrection and the arrival of the Messianic Era. In that regard, the manifestation of the Holy Spirit upon the disciples served as an early sign of the coming new covenant.

WALKING BY THE SPIRIT

In many circles of faith, people think of the gift of the Holy Spirit only in terms of supernatural abilities such as performing miracles, uttering prophecies, discerning spirits, speaking in unknown languages, and other types of spiritual manifestations. The Spirit of God does sometimes manifest in supernatural miracles, but that's not the reason that God imparts his Spirit to the disciples of Yeshua. He gives his Spirit as earnest money, so to speak, to function as a down payment on the promises yet to come in the Messianic Era.

According to the prophets, the LORD will pour out his Holy Spirit on all people in the Messianic Era. The LORD says, "I will pour out my Spirit on all flesh; your sons and your daughters shall prophesy, your old men shall dream dreams, and your young men shall see visions. Even on the male and female servants in those days I will pour out my Spirit." (Joel 3:1–2 [2:28–29]). This will be part of the universal revelation of God in the Messianic Era. Another prophecy from Ezekiel explains that the LORD will pour out his Spirit in order to change our inner nature:

> I will give you a new heart, and a new spirit I will put within you. And I will remove the heart of stone from your flesh and give you a heart of flesh. And I will put my Spirit within you, and cause you to walk in my statutes and be careful to obey my rules. (Ezekiel 36:26–27)

The Prophet Isaiah says that in the Messianic Era, "Your ears shall hear a word behind you, saying, 'This is the way, walk in it,' when you turn to the right or when you turn to the left" (Isaiah 30:21). Then the people will renounce their sins. In other words, whenever a person starts to turn astray, turning away from the straight and narrow path, either to the left or to the right, the Spirit will correct him, saying, "No, this is the way; walk this way." That's what it means to walk in the Spirit. That's what the Spirit-led life looks like.

Paul alludes to these prophecies when he says to the Gentile disciples of Galatia, "Walk by the Spirit, and you will not gratify the desires of the flesh" (Galatians 5:16). He instructed the Gentile disciples to walk by the Spirit rather than gratifying the desires of the body. The instruction to "walk by the Spirit" alludes directly to the words from Ezekiel: "I will put my Spirit within you, and cause you to walk in my statutes and be careful to obey my rules." The one who walks according to the Spirit will walk in God's statutes and obey his rules. Even though the Messianic Era has not yet arrived, and the New Covenant Era has not yet begun, the apostles taught that disciples of Yeshua have already received an advance portion of the Holy Spirit as a down payment. Therefore, we can begin to take advantage of this prophecy right now. We can opt to walk by God's Spirit and keep his laws today.

This discussion should make it clear that the apostles did not place the Spirit in antithesis to the Torah as the replacement theology interpretation does. From the apostolic perspective, the Holy Spirit and the Torah fit hand and glove. To pit the Spirit against the laws of the Torah creates a false dichotomy. If there is a dichotomy at work, it's the contrast between our human physical inclinations (the flesh) and the leading of God's Spirit:

> The desires of the flesh are against the Spirit, and the desires of the Spirit are against the flesh, for these are opposed to each other, to keep you from doing the things you want to do. (Galatians 5:17)

Our mortal human inclination is errant. In other words, human beings are naturally naughty. From the days of Noah, "the LORD saw that the wickedness of man was great in the earth, and that every intention of the thoughts of his heart was only evil continually" (Genesis 6:5). Even when we do not want to sin, we find ourselves doing so. Human bodies and human minds rebel against God's authority. The disciple trying to follow God's righteousness experiences a war within his heart—a mental battle for his thoughts, speech, and behaviors. Judaism employs a similar concept, dividing the human psyche into an evil inclination and a good inclination. The two inclinations war within the mind for mastery.

THE TORAH OF MESSIAH

In his book *Love and the Messianic Age*, Paul Philip Levertoff says, "In the days of the Messiah the inner nature of God will be revealed, and His light will permeate man." Everyone will know God, from the least of them to the greatest of them. In the Messianic Era, "your Teacher will not hide himself anymore, but your eyes shall see your Teacher" (Isaiah 30:20), and "all flesh will see [him] together" (Isaiah 40:5). The Messiah will reveal the Inner Torah to humanity in a universal revelation of godliness and heightened awareness of the LORD. Then, the Torah will go out from Zion. All nations will ascend to Messianic Jerusalem to learn Torah from the Messiah, and, according to the rabbis, "the Messiah will elucidate for them the words of the Torah ... and he will correct errors in its interpretation" (*Genesis Rabbah* 98:9). The rabbis also say that the Messiah will teach a "new Torah," the Torah of Messiah. The Messiah's "new Torah will go forth" to all nations, as it says, "A Torah will go forth from Me, and I will set My justice for a light of the peoples" (Isaiah 51:4 my translation; *Leviticus Rabbah* 13:3).

The sages said that the new Torah of Messiah will reveal the supernal Torah—the hidden will and wisdom of God. By comparison, if the Torah of Moses were likened to a human body, the Torah of Messiah would be the divine soul that animates the body. Like the Temple on earth reflecting the heavenly Sanctuary, the Torah of Moses merely reflects the supernal Torah. It translates the heavenly revelation of God's will and wisdom into the language of human beings. When the Torah of Messiah comes, it will reveal the original heavenly version.

A seventeenth-century kabbalist quoted in Raphael Patai's *The Messiah Texts* puts it this way:

> Just as the children of man will divest themselves of the [mortal] body, so the Torah will be divested of her bodily aspect, and her hidden face will radiate, and the righteous will occupy themselves with her. (Avraham Azulai, *Chesed l'Avraham*)

Paul says that if the Torah of Moses came with glory, the new Torah will come with even greater glory: "Indeed, in this case, what once had glory has come to have no glory at all, because of the glory that surpasses it" (2 Corinthians 3:10). That is to say that the glory of the Torah of Messiah will be so great that, by comparison, it will seem as if the Torah of Moses had none. The sages say something similar: "The Torah which a man learns in this world is like nothing in comparison to the Torah of the Messiah" (*Ecclesiastes Rabbah* 11:8).

The idea of a new Torah might seem like a problem. According to the Bible, the Torah that God gave through Moses at Mount Sinai is eternal. Yeshua said, "Do not think that I came to abolish the Torah ... For truly I say to you, until heaven and earth pass away, not the smallest letter or stroke shall pass from the Torah until all is accomplished" (Matthew 5:17-18). If that is the case, then how can he bring a new Torah?

The rabbis explain that the new Torah of Messiah is not a different Torah—it's the same Torah, but the Messiah will reveal the inner meanings of the Torah. He will open the spiritual dimensions of the Torah of Moses to show us the things hidden within it. Rabbi Levi Yitzchak of Berdichev (1740-1809) says that the Messiah will even explain the white spaces between the letters of the Torah. Yosef Yitzchak Schneersohn (1880-1950), the sixth Lubavitcher Rebbe, says it this way:

> "A Torah will go forth from Me" (Isaiah 51:4). This means that the Holy One, blessed be He, said, "A New Torah from me will go forth." This is not to say that the Torah will be changed (God forbid), for the Torah is eternal. Rather, the Holy One,

blessed be He, will reveal new insights into the Torah which have never been revealed. He will reveal things which were covered and concealed from Moses, our teacher (peace be upon him), and from the forefathers. In this New Torah, the reasons for the commandments, which are concealed from us now, will all be revealed ... The Messiah will reveal to us the true, inner, spiritual meaning of the commandments, the inner facets of the Torah ... which were hidden and concealed from Moses. (*Sefer Hamaamorim, 5699*)

According to this explanation, the new Torah of Messiah is the same Torah that Moses received at Mount Sinai: "The Torah will be divested of her bodily aspect ... but the Torah herself is one for all eternity, she will always remain what she was, and will stand for ever, and will not change, God forbid!" (*Chesed l'Avraham*). The new Torah will be the same Torah, but the Messiah will present new dimensions and worlds of understanding that lie hidden within it.

BENEATH THE TORAH'S VEIL

The mystics explain that the Torah that Israel received at Mount Sinai is only an outer shell (so to speak) of the true, supernal revelation that God sent into the world "on the third day." According to this idea, the revelation at Sinai included much more than just the Ten Commandments. It included the whole Torah, and not just the written Torah, but also all the prophecies of the prophets and every revelation that God would ever deliver to mankind. Even those prophets who had not yet been born received their revelations at Sinai, as it says, "It is not with you alone that I am making this sworn covenant, but with whoever is standing here with us today before the LORD our God, and with whoever is not here with us today" (Deuteronomy 29:14–15). Yosef Yitzchak Schneersohn says:

> Even the Torah of Messiah [which will be revealed in the Messianic Era] was already given at Mount Sinai, and the children of Israel learned it, as it says, "on the third day." This indicates the concept that even the Torah of Messiah was given then. (*Sefer Hamaamorim, 5730*)

In the Messianic Era, new light will shine on Zion from out of Zion. The nations will walk by that light, and they will ascend to Zion to learn God's ways. The written Torah we possess today is only an earthly incarnation, so to speak, of God's supernal will and wisdom. The Torah, as we know it, translates God's will and wisdom into the language of men and the rubrics of this current age. One might say that the physical Torah we possess in this world, written with ink on a scroll, is a copy and a shadow of the unseen eternal Torah.

In the future, the Spirit of God (which is already, in some small measure, at work within us) will write the supernal Torah on our hearts, replacing our hearts of stone with hearts of flesh and causing us to walk in his statutes and obey his laws.

THE INNER WAR IN ROMANS 7–8

We have not yet attained this Inner Torah that the Spirit places within us. We have received a small down payment, not the whole sum. This explains the difficult material that Paul presents in Romans 7–8. In these chapters, Paul argues that even though Gentile disciples are not "under the Law" in the manner of the Jewish disciples, they should nonetheless conduct themselves under the authority of the Spirit. The following short study of Romans 7–8 detours from our study in the book of Hebrews, but it will help us understand the practical ramifications and outworking of the new covenant in the here and now. The detour begins in Romans 7:15 where Paul expresses the inner tension he experiences between spirit and flesh.

WHY I DO NOT DO WHAT I WANT TO DO

> I do not understand my own actions. For I do not do what I want, but I do the very thing I hate. Now if I do what I do not want, I agree with the law, that it is good. So now it is no longer I who do it, but sin that dwells within me. For I know that nothing good dwells in me, that is, in my flesh. For I have the desire to do what is right, but not the ability to carry it out. (Romans 7:15-18)

In angst over his own sins and shortcomings, the apostle explains that every human being is captive to sin. The evil inclination and physical mind strive in rebellion against God's Torah. Disciples of Yeshua have not yet reached the place where the Torah is already written on our hearts. The desire to live righteously according to the Torah's commandments has been planted in their hearts. The disciple wants to live out God's instruction and obey his commandments, but he has not yet been given the supernatural ability to do so. Paul says, "I do not do the good I want, but the evil I do not want is what I keep on doing" (Romans 7:19).

The disciple feels discouraged from time to time in his or her struggle with sin and temptation. Even the holy Apostle Paul felt discouraged. He said, "Now if I do what I do not want, it is no longer I who do it, but sin that dwells within me. So I find it to be a law that when I want to do right, evil lies close at hand" (Romans 7:20–21).

The apostle further explains that his inner being (the *neshamah*) delights in the Torah, but his wayward flesh and evil inclination are in rebellion against the Torah: "I delight in the law of God, in my inner being" (Romans 7:22). The "Torah of God," in which Paul's inner being delights is not a new spiritual Torah dictated by the subjective whims of his personal conscience, it's the Torah of Moses. He delights in it in his inner being because the Spirit of God is already at work in him, writing it upon his heart. But at the same time, another spirit remains at work with him.

THE LAW OF SIN

> I see in my members another law waging war against the law of my mind and making me captive to the law of sin that dwells in my members. Wretched man that I am! Who will deliver me from this body of death? Thanks be to God through [Yeshua the Messiah our Master]! So then, I myself serve the law of God with my mind, but with my flesh I serve the law of sin. (Romans 7:23–25)

These admissions indicate that we have not yet arrived at the fulfillment of the new covenant. Paul admits that he still struggles with sin, and he does not do the good he wants to do. He endures an inner struggle between the Torah and sin. He looks forward to the redemption when God will set him free from the mortal body that is so tightly bound to sin. He looks forward to the promise of the new covenant.

In this present world, Israel remains under the old covenant—the agreement to keep the Torah—but human beings continually break that agreement. The new covenant will be the covenant for the Messianic Era and the World to Come.

In the Messianic Era, the Holy Spirit of God will place his supernal Torah within us and write his will and wisdom directly onto our hearts. There will be no barrier between us and his holy will. Imagine a day when our spirit and our flesh and all of our inclinations agree to serve God in complete unity. No more inner battle.

If I were to quit reading at the end of Romans 7, I might conclude, "In that case, I'm off the hook. I'm a sinner, just like Paul. Sin lives in me, and I have received only a deposit of the Holy Spirit, so what can I do about my sinful nature? In the future, God will make me a righteous person, but for now, I'm content to be a sinner saved by grace." Lest we leave off with that impression, we have to keep reading a short way into the next chapter of the epistle.

THE LAW OF SIN AND DEATH

> There is therefore now no condemnation for those who are in [the Messiah Yeshua]. For the law of the Spirit of life has set you free in [the Messiah Yeshua] from the law of sin and death. (Romans 8:1-2)

The disciple of Yeshua need not fear condemnation on the day of judgment because if he walks according to the Spirit, he will not suffer the consequences of the law of sin and death. Many teachers wrongly equate "the law of sin and death" with the Torah. On the contrary, the law of sin and death is the simple spiritual rule articulated in Romans 6:23: "For the wages of sin is death." Sin begets death. This law has been in place since the garden of Eden (Genesis 2:17), long before the Torah of Moses entered the world at Sinai. The disciple in whom the Spirit is at work has been set free from those consequences because he walks according to "the law of the Spirit of life," a simple spiritual rule articulated in Romans 6:23: "The free gift of God is eternal life in [the Messiah Yeshua] our Lord."

- Law of sin and death = The wages of sin is death.
- Law of the Spirit of life = The free gift of God is eternal life in the Messiah Yeshua.

LICENSE TO SIN

> God has done what the law, weakened by the flesh, could not do. By sending his own Son in the likeness of sinful flesh and for sin, he condemned sin in the flesh, in order that the righteous requirement of the law might be fulfilled in us, who walk not according to the flesh but according to the Spirit. (Romans 8:3–4)

The Torah is unable to offer eternal life because it is "weakened by the flesh" in that human beings commit sins, consigning them to the law of sin and death. The law of the Spirit of life depends on the righteous merit of Yeshua for eternal life, not the merit of the sinner. Nevertheless, the law of the Spirit of life is not a license to sin. Instead, the Messiah "condemned sin" so that the disciple might fulfill "the righteous requirement of the Torah" by walking according to the Spirit. Until the final redemption, the disciple experiences an ongoing struggle against his own body (the flesh) and against sin. However, the ongoing struggle does not excuse him to "sin and sin boldly" or to fatalistically resign himself to helplessly succumb to sin's seductions. The disciple has already received the deposit of the Holy Spirit. The disciple has received a foretaste of the Spirit, a downpayment on the new covenant and the new life. If we experience a measure of the future kingdom now, our final victory and verdict are assured at the time of the redemption. Therefore, every disciple is obligated to walk according to the Spirit and not according to the physical inclinations of the flesh. We lay hold of the future Messianic Era and the promises of the new covenant even though that future has not yet arrived.

THE SPIRIT AND THE FLESH

> Those who live according to the flesh set their minds on the things of the flesh, but those who live according to the Spirit set their minds on the things of the Spirit. For to set the mind on the flesh is death, but to set the mind on the Spirit is life and peace. For the mind that is set on the flesh is hostile to God, for it does not submit to God's law; indeed, it cannot. Those who are in the flesh cannot please God. (Romans 8:5-8)

If we let sin rule us, we live in hostility to God and rebellion against his Torah. The one who lives according to the Spirit strives to fulfill the righteous requirement of the Torah on the basis of the new spiritual life birthed within. The one living by the flesh is not even trying. His mind is "set on the flesh," that is, on how to gratify the various physical desires and vanities of his body in this present world. One who lives only for the pleasures of this present world has set his mind on death because the things of this world are temporary. "Those who live according to the Spirit" conduct their lives according to the dictates of the Spirit rather than the dictates of the flesh. They set their minds "on the things of the Spirit," such as the future kingdom, the reward of the righteous, the resurrection of the dead, and eternal life.

> You, however, are not in the flesh but in the Spirit, if in fact the Spirit of God dwells in you. Anyone who does not have the Spirit of [Messiah] does not belong to him. But if [Messiah] is in you, although the body is dead because of sin, the Spirit is life because of righteousness. (Romans 8:9-10)

The disciple is under obligation to the Spirit, not the flesh. If a disciple conducts himself according to the flesh and not the Spirit, that indicates an absence of the Spirit of the Messiah. Such a person does not belong to the Messiah. If the Spirit of the Messiah is within the disciple, the person will experience a war between life and death within him. The body and its desires represent death, but the Spirit and its righteousness represent life. The body of death and the Spirit of life remain locked in a fierce wrestling match, like Jacob and Esau wrestling in the womb of Rebekah, until judgment day and trumpets sound. When those trumpets do sound, the battle will be over. Until then, the disciple walking according to the Spirit continually exercises vigilance and repentance lest sin prevail.

THE WORK OF THE SPIRIT

> If the Spirit of him who raised [Yeshua] from the dead dwells in you, he who raised [the Messiah Yeshua] from the dead will also give life to your mortal bodies through his Spirit who dwells in you. So then, brothers, we are debtors, not to the flesh, to live according to the flesh. For if you live according to the flesh you will die, but if by the Spirit you put to death the deeds of the body, you will live. For all who are led by the Spirit of God are sons of God. (Romans 8:11–14)

The one who walks according to the Spirit possesses "the Spirit of him who raised [Yeshua] from the dead." That same Spirit will raise the disciple. In this regard, every disciple has received a spiritual advance on the glory and revelation of the Messianic Era. We have received the Spirit of God as a deposit, not to give us a new, easier, less-rigid standard of righteousness in our hearts, but to begin the process of placing the supernal Torah of God—his will and wisdom—within us. The Spirit does not excuse us from obedience; the Spirit reprograms us for obedience. If we give up the fight and decide to wait until the resurrection and regeneration before walking in righteousness, then we opt to live according to the flesh and not the Spirit. "If you live according to the flesh you will die." The one who lives by the Spirit is actively repenting by putting "to death the deeds of the body." Such a person will inherit eternal life.

The Spirit removes the heart of stone and replaces it with a heart soft and pliable on which God may write his Torah, as it says, "These words that I command you today shall be on your heart." We are to conduct ourselves as citizens of the coming kingdom, living according to the dictates of the Messianic Era and not according to this present world. We are under obligation to the future kingdom of heaven and not the kingdom of darkness that prevails in this current age. We are obligated to live in a manner worthy of the new covenant.

STOP SIGNS IN THE KINGDOM

Let's return to the stop sign analogy. Suppose that the Torah contained a commandment to bring your vehicle to a complete stop whenever you arrive at an intersection with a stop sign. Under the newness of the Spirit, you will stop at the intersection, not just because of the stop sign and not because you fear a traffic ticket but because it's the right and legal thing to do. The Spirit will write "STOP" on your heart:

> Your ears shall hear a word behind you, saying, "This is the *stop sign; stop at it," before* you turn to the right or to the left. (Isaiah 30:21, paraphrased to make a point)

Under the newness of the Spirit, you will know the right thing to do, and you will want to do it. Moreover, in the Messianic Era, you won't even feel tempted to run the stop sign or to ease through it without coming to a complete stop. Through the revelation of the new Torah of Messiah, you will understand the reason for stopping at the stop sign, and you will even understand the meaning of the spaces between the letters in the word "stop."

We have not yet arrived at that point. Although the Spirit is at work within us, writing "STOP" on our hearts, it's not yet finished. Our evil inclination is still alive and mostly unfettered, and it doesn't want to stop. We make up excuses and justifications, such as, "Since I realize that the intention of the law is only to prevent collisions, I need not stop in the absence of other traffic." Or perhaps we say, "I will stop, but the Spirit frees me from the letter so that I don't need to come to a complete stop. I can just ease through the intersection." Two voices struggle within us: the old man and the new man. Both try to control the vehicle. When the redemption comes, the struggle will be over, but that does not free us from heeding the law now.

Inasmuch as you live according to the "newness of the Spirit," you will be living a godly life consistent with the literal commandments of the Torah, as they apply to you as a Gentile or as they apply to you as a Jew.

CHAPTER FOUR
BETTER PROMISES

The Bible speaks of an old covenant and a new covenant. According to the book of Hebrews, the new covenant offers better promises than the old. Yeshua is the mediator of the new covenant. He "has obtained a ministry that is as much more excellent than the old as the covenant he mediates is better, since it is enacted on better promises" (Hebrews 8:6). What are the better promises of this new covenant?

In the last few chapters, we have learned that contrary to popular opinion, the old covenant is not the same thing as the Old Testament or the Law. The old covenant is the agreement between God and the nation of Israel. For his part, God promised to take Israel as his people, and for their part, the people of Israel promised to behave themselves and keep the commandments of the Torah as a matter of covenant fidelity. That agreement between God and Israel constitutes the old covenant.

The new covenant is not the same thing as the New Testament. The new covenant is not just another way of saying Christianity. The new covenant has not yet arrived in its fullness. The new covenant is a new agreement for the Messianic Era. According to the terms of the new covenant, God will change his people by placing his Torah within them and writing its laws on their hearts.

What are the better promises of the new covenant? Identifying the better promises requires some Bible study, starting, of course, in the new covenant—not the New Testament but the new covenant as presented in the prophecies of Jeremiah.

DAY OF THE LORD

> "Behold, the days are coming," declares the LORD. (Jeremiah 31:31)

When the prophets preface their oracle with the statement, "The day is coming," or "The days are coming," or "In that day," such formulas indicate that the ensuing prophecy pertains to the end of days, the final redemption, the Messianic Era, and the Day of the LORD. As the rabbis said, "All the prophets prophesied only for the days of Messiah."

When Jeremiah says, "Behold, the days are coming," we immediately know he has the final redemption in view. To put it another way, he is talking about the end times. This should alert us to a problem with the theology that teaches the new covenant has already replaced the old covenant and that Christ has canceled the Torah. The new covenant is a covenant for the future eschaton, and that has not happened yet.

WITH THE JEWISH PEOPLE

> When I will make a new covenant with the house of Israel and the house of Judah. (Jeremiah 31:31)

The LORD says he will make the new covenant with the house of Israel and the house of Judah, that is, the Jewish people. This indicates that the new covenant is like the old one in that it will be a covenant between two parties: God and the Jewish people. The words "a new covenant with the house of Israel and with the house of Judah" do not mean "a new covenant with Christians" or "a new covenant with Gentiles." It does not mention Gentiles at all. This creates a problem for Gentiles. The non-Jew is not a party to the new covenant. The nations are not part of the agreement. The new covenant, like the old covenant, pertains exclusively to the relationship between God and Israel. The only covenant that the nations have with God is the covenant that God made with Noah, his sons, and all the animals.

This realization turns conventional ideas about the new covenant completely around. Replacement theology insists that if a Jew wants to enter the kingdom, he must renounce his allegiance to Judaism and become a Christian, leaving behind his Jewish identity and allegiance to the Torah. The terms of the new covenant imply the opposite. If a Gentile wants to receive benefit from the new covenant, he or she needs to find some avenue of participation with the Jewish people because it's a national covenant exclusive to the house of Judah and Israel.

Did the tables just turn?

THE BROKEN COVENANT

> Not like the covenant that I made with their fathers on the day when I took them by the hand to bring them out of the land of Egypt, my covenant that they broke, though I was their husband, declares the LORD. (Jeremiah 31:32)

The old covenant has been broken for a long time. Forty days after Israel agreed to the terms of the old covenant, the people broke those terms by creating an idol and worshiping it. Moses shattered the tablets of the covenant, symbolizing that Israel had broken the covenant.

That wasn't the only time. Every sin committed by the nation breaches the terms of the covenant. The Levitical priesthood had the job of performing continual, daily covenant maintenance to compensate for such breaches, repair the relationship, and keep the covenant viable. The LORD compares the relationship to a marriage. He says, "I was their husband." The prophets often depict the nation as the bride of God. When the nation indulges in idolatry, the prophets compare it to adultery. Under the terms of the covenant, such infidelities eventually accumulate to the point that God punishes the nation with exile from the land. The Greek translation (LXX) of Jeremiah (quoted in Hebrews 8:9) uses strong language to indicate God's displeasure with the unfaithful bride: "For they did not remain in my covenant, so I disregarded them."

TORAH ON THE HEARTS

> This is the covenant that I will make with the house of Israel after those days, declares the LORD: I will put my law within them, and I will write it on their hearts. (Jeremiah 31:33)

The new covenant is "not like the covenant I made with their fathers," which can result in exile and punishment for the nation. It's not just a renewed version of the old. It's something new and, apparently, based on better promises than the old.

The better promises begin with the promise of transforming the people. God is going to put his Torah within his people. He promises to write his Torah on their hearts. This is a better promise than the terms the old covenant offered. Whereas the old covenant simply set a standard of righteousness that the nation needed to meet, this new arrangement promises to make the individual members of the nation righteous so that they can meet the standards.

THE HOLY MARRIAGE

> I will be their God, and they shall be my people. (Jeremiah 31:33)

Under the terms of the new covenant, the LORD will be the God of Israel, and Israel will be his people. He made the same promise when he promised to take Israel from Egypt (Exodus 6:7), and he reiterated the offer at Sinai (Exodus 19:5). The formula sounds matrimonial. In an ancient Near Eastern wedding, the husband made a legal statement, declaring over his bride, "I will be your husband, and you shall be my wife." The better promises of the new covenant promise that the relationship will be restored. It predicts a future redemption of the nation and the ultimate consummation of the relationship between God and his people. The LORD will seal his relationship with the Jewish people like the union between a husband and a wife.

KNOWLEDGE OF THE LORD

> No longer shall each one teach his neighbor and each his brother, saying, "Know the LORD," for they shall all know me, from the least of them to the greatest, declares the LORD. (Jeremiah 31:34)

The new covenant includes a universal revelation of the LORD. Every Jew will know the truth and have an intimate and personal knowledge of the Almighty. Knowledge of God is not merely knowledge about God; it implies a relationship with God. The concept is closely connected with the idea of the fear of the LORD:

- The fear of the LORD is the beginning of knowledge. (Proverbs 1:7)
- Then, you will understand the fear of the LORD and find the knowledge of God. (Proverbs 2:5)
- The fear of the LORD is the beginning of wisdom, and the knowledge of the Holy One is insight. (Proverbs 9:10)

In the days of Jeremiah, prophets like him were on a perpetual mission to teach their neighbors and their brothers, saying, "Know the LORD." It was a constant struggle to persuade the nation to fear God. They continually called on the people to repent, just as preachers and Bible teachers do to this very day. The Prophet Hosea complained, "There is no faithfulness or steadfast love, and *no knowledge of God* in the land; there is swearing, lying, murder, stealing, and committing adultery; they break all bounds, and bloodshed follows bloodshed" (Hosea 4:1-2). A similar complaint about clergy and religious leaders appears in the early chapters of Jeremiah:

> The priests did not say, "Where is the LORD?" Those who handle the law *did not know me*; the shepherds transgressed against me; the prophets prophesied by Baal and went after things that do not profit. (Jeremiah 2:8, emphasis mine)

The prophecy complains that even the priests, the teachers of the Torah, and the prophets did not know the LORD. They obviously did know about the LORD. But they did not know him.

In the Messianic Era, all Israel, from the least to the greatest, will receive universal revelation of God, and they will all know the LORD. It means that people will conduct their lives and all their affairs in the fear of the LORD. That's one of those better promises that has not yet been fulfilled on planet earth.

FORGIVENESS OF SINS

> I will forgive their iniquity, and I will remember their sin no more. (Jeremiah 31:34)

Under the new covenant, the LORD will forgive the sins of the house of Judah and the house of Israel. He will pardon the sins of the nation.

They will be remembered no more. This is certainly a better promise of the new covenant.

Complete absolution means an end to exile. Under the terms of the old covenant's curses and blessings (Leviticus 26; Deuteronomy 28), God must punish the nation's transgressions, and if the nation fails to repent, he must send them into exile. In the future, when the nation's sins are forgiven and their iniquities are no longer remembered, there will be no need for punishment, no chastisement, no curses, and no more exile for the Jewish people. Forgiveness of sins clears the way for the final redemption. This is yet another of the better promises of the new covenant.

AN ETERNAL NATION

> Thus says the LORD, who gives the sun for light by day and the fixed order of the moon and the stars for light by night, who stirs up the sea so that its waves roar—the LORD of hosts is his name: "If this fixed order departs from before me, declares the LORD, then shall the offspring of Israel cease from being a nation before me forever." (Jeremiah 31:35-36)

As long as the sun, moon, and stars are above, so long as the heavenly bodies continue in their courses, and as long as the sea is bound to wash upon the sand, the Jewish people will never cease from being a nation before God. This is one of the better promises of the new covenant. The promise implies that the Jewish people will continue as a distinct, separate, and identifiable people group into the Messianic Era. The Jewish people will continue as a nation with their own national sovereignty. Jeremiah did not have the modern State of Israel in view. Instead, the prophecy refers to the government of King Messiah, as Isaiah predicted:

> Of the increase of his government and of peace there will be no end, on the throne of David and over his kingdom, to establish it and to uphold it with justice and with righteousness from this time forth and forevermore. The zeal of the LORD of hosts will do this. (Isaiah 9:7)

NEVER ABANDONED OR REPLACED

> Thus says the LORD: "If the heavens above can be measured, and the foundations of the earth below can be explored, then I will cast off all the offspring of Israel for all that they have done, declares the LORD." (Jeremiah 31:37)

Replacement theology teaches that the LORD has rejected and abandoned the Jewish people because they did not accept the messianic claims of Jesus. Replacement theology denies the Jewish people have any ongoing covenant relationship with the LORD. Unless they become Christians, they are destined only for damnation because Christianity has replaced the Jewish religion, and Christians have replaced the Jewish people as the people of God. The better promises of the new covenant, however, state that the LORD will reject the nation of Israel and cast them off for their sin only "if the heavens can be measured, and the foundations … explored." It's a rhetorical point: The heavens above cannot be measured, and the foundations of the earth below cannot be explored. Therefore, the LORD will never reject the Jewish people or cast them off for their sins. After the final redemption, there will never be another exile. Otherwise the final redemption would not be final, would it?

AN ETERNAL CITY

> Behold, the days are coming, declares the LORD, when the city shall be rebuilt for the LORD from the Tower of Hananel to the Corner Gate. And the measuring line shall go out farther, straight to the hill Gareb, and shall then turn to Goah. The whole valley of the dead bodies and the ashes, and all the fields as far as the brook Kidron, to the corner of the Horse Gate toward the east, shall be sacred to the LORD. It shall not be uprooted or overthrown anymore forever. (Jeremiah 31:35–40)

The better promises of the new covenant state that, in the Messianic Era, the LORD will rebuild the holy city of Jerusalem as an everlasting city, never to be destroyed again. Messianic Jerusalem, the new Zion, will be the capital city of the world. The entire city will be holy to the LORD.

Ironically, the LORD gave these promises to Jeremiah while the Babylonian siege was already underway: "At that time the army of the king of Babylon was besieging Jerusalem, and Jeremiah the prophet was shut up in the court of the guard that was in the palace of the king of Judah" (Jeremiah 32:2). As the destruction of Jerusalem commenced, the LORD predicted a future day when the city would be rebuilt and never destroyed again. That day has not yet come. The Romans destroyed the city of Jerusalem just forty years after the ascension of the Master, another indication that his death and resurrection did not signify the onset of the new covenant era. If it had, Jerusalem would never have fallen again. When the Messiah returns, however, he will rebuild Jerusalem as an everlasting city.

INGATHERING AND SECURITY

> Behold, I will gather them from all the countries to which I drove them in my anger and my wrath and in great indignation. I will bring them back to this place, and I will make them dwell in safety. And they shall be my people, and I will be their God. (Jeremiah 32:37-38)

As Nebuchadnezzar's armies laid siege to Jerusalem, the LORD told Jeremiah to buy a piece of property in Judah to indicate that, in the future, "houses and fields and vineyards shall again be bought in this land" (Jeremiah 32:15). Jeremiah objected to the idea of purchasing a field in the middle of a siege. The LORD replied by rattling off several more of the "better promises" of the new covenant, including the better promise to gather the exiles of Israel back to the land of Israel and plant them back in their land.

In the Messianic Era, the LORD will bring the scattered Jewish people back to the land of their forefathers, and they will "dwell in safety." In our day, many Jewish people have already returned to the land of Israel, but they certainly do not "dwell in safety." When the LORD gathers Israel, he will grant them security in their own land.

ONE HEART

> I will give them one heart and one way, that they may fear me forever, for their own good and the good of their children after them. (Jeremiah 32:39)

The better promises of the new covenant state that the LORD will unite the Jewish people. He will give them "one heart and one way." No longer will the Jewish people be divided among themselves. They will be united in their fear of the LORD and their service to him. No longer will the people stray from the service of the LORD. Their children and grandchildren will reap the benefits of their newfound unity and their steadfast fear of the LORD.

EVERLASTING COVENANT

> I will make with them an everlasting covenant, that I will not turn away from doing good to them. And I will put the fear of me in their hearts, that they may not turn from me. (Jeremiah 32:40)

The better promises of the everlasting new covenant state that the LORD will not turn away from the Jewish people, and the Jewish people will not turn away from him. In order to ensure that they never do turn away from him again, he will put the fear of the LORD in their hearts—an idea equivalent to writing his Torah on their hearts. The covenant he makes with them at that time will be an everlasting covenant, never to be broken by either party.

PLANTED IN THE LAND

> I will rejoice in doing them good, and I will plant them in this land in faithfulness, with all my heart and all my soul. For thus says the LORD: Just as I have brought all this great disaster upon this people, so I will bring upon them all the good that I promise them. Fields shall be bought in this land. (Jeremiah 32:41–43)

The better promises of the new covenant state that, in the time to come, the LORD will plant his people back in their land, and he will fix his attention on them and attend to them "with all my heart and all my soul." Just as he punished them with disaster, deportations, and exile, he will rejoice to do good for them, reversing all those misfortunes. Then property will be bought and sold again in the land of Israel. That's why the LORD wanted Jeremiah to buy a field.

THE BRANCH OF DAVID

> Behold, the days are coming, declares the LORD, when I will fulfill the promise I made to the house of Israel and the house of Judah. In those days and at that time I will cause a righteous Branch to spring up for David, and he shall execute justice and righteousness in the land. (Jeremiah 33:14-15)

The better promises of the new covenant state that the LORD will "cause a righteous Branch to spring up for David." A king from the house of David will take the throne of David and administer over the land, doing righteousness and bringing justice. After that, "David shall never lack a man to sit on the throne of the house of Israel" (Jeremiah 33:17). The "righteous Branch" is King Messiah. Jerusalem will be his capital city. He will save Judah and bring security to Jerusalem. Then the city will be called, "The LORD is our righteousness" (Jeremiah 33:16). These specific messianic expectations cannot be derived from the terms of the old covenant. These are new covenant promises that have not yet been fulfilled. They are a promise of what is to come.

PRIESTHOOD AND TEMPLE

> The Levitical priests shall never lack a man in my presence to offer burnt offerings, to burn grain offerings, and to make sacrifices forever. (Jeremiah 33:18)

The LORD promises that, under the new covenant, the Temple will be rebuilt, and the Levitical priesthood will conduct the worship and the sacrificial services prescribed by the Torah. Replacement theology teaches that the new-covenant priesthood of Messiah replaces the old covenant's Levitical priesthood, and the new-covenant sacrifice of Yeshua replaces the old covenant's animal sacrifices. According to the better promises of the new covenant, the LORD will reinstate the

Temple, the sacrifices, and the Levitical priesthood in the Messianic Era, which leads us to ask, "What about the sacrifices?"

Despite objections from theology, the LORD is emphatic about the restoration of the Temple and the Levitical priesthood:

> Thus says the LORD: If you can break my covenant with the day and my covenant with the night, so that day and night will not come at their appointed time, then also my covenant with David my servant may be broken, so that he shall not have a son to reign on his throne, and my covenant with the Levitical priests my ministers. (Jeremiah 33:20–21)

So long as the earth continues to spin, two things will be certain: the Davidic heir (King Messiah) will occupy the throne of David, and Aaronic heirs (the Levitical priesthood) will serve in the restored Temple. Despite objections from replacement theology, the LORD is emphatic about the restoration of the Temple and the Levitical priesthood. The prophecy places the "covenant with the Levitical priests" on the same par as the covenant with David. That puts the future reinstatement of the priesthood on the same level of priority as the Messiah's occupation of the Davidic throne during the Messianic Era. The house of David will have King Messiah reigning on his throne, and the house of Aaron will have Levitical priests serving in the Temple. The two function in tandem, not in competition with one another. According to this prophecy, it's impossible to instate the Davidic Messiah while simultaneously discarding the Levitical priesthood. That should give pause to the assumptions of replacement theology, which teach that the Messiah abrogates the Levitical system. The "better promises" of the new covenant demand the ongoing role of the Aaronic priesthood.

> As the host of heaven cannot be numbered and the sands of the sea cannot be measured, so I will multiply the offspring of David my servant, and the Levitical priests who minister to me. (Jeremiah 33:22)

The better promises of the new covenant promise a proliferation of the seed of David and the number of Levitical priests qualified to serve in the priesthood. The prophecy ensures that there will always be plenty of candidates available to fill those offices. The house of David will never lack a qualified heir to occupy the throne; the house of Aaron will never lack a sufficient number of qualified men for the priesthood.

NO LONGER A NATION

> The word of the LORD came to Jeremiah: "Have you not observed that these people are saying, 'The LORD has rejected the two clans that he chose'? Thus they have despised my people so that they are no longer a nation in their sight." (Jeremiah 33:23-24)

The better promises of the new covenant state that God will never replace his people with another or break his covenants with "the two clans that he chose," i.e., the house of David and the house of Aaron. In view of these better promises, the assumptions of replacement theology sound especially ironic. For nearly two thousand years, we have been told that, under the new covenant, God has rejected Israel and the Levitical priesthood.

In the face of the impending destruction of Jerusalem and the fall of the Davidic monarchy, the nations in Jeremiah's day also wrote off the Jewish people. Judah's enemies dismissed the house of David and the house of Aaron as obsolete. They cynically said, "The LORD has rejected the two clans that he chose." In other words, they claimed that the LORD would no longer honor his promises to the house of David and the house of Aaron. Moreover, they despised the Jewish people and no longer considered them to be a viable nation. Ironically, replacement theology makes the same claims. We have been taught the cancellation of the Levitical priesthood and a complete dismissal of both the national aspirations and covenant status of the Jewish people. We have been taught that the Jewish people are no longer God's elect and that the Levitical priesthood has no further role to play, thus contradicting the "better promises" of the new covenant.

UNTIL HEAVEN AND EARTH PASS AWAY

> Thus says the LORD: If I have not established my covenant with day and night and the fixed order of heaven and earth, then I will reject the offspring of Jacob and David my servant and will not choose one of his offspring to rule over the offspring of Abraham, Isaac, and Jacob. For I will restore their fortunes and will have mercy on them. (Jeremiah 33:25–26)

The better promises of the new covenant state that God will restore the Jewish people, the offspring of Abraham, Isaac, and Jacob. He will restore their fortunes and have mercy on them. He will never reject the offspring of Jacob (the Jewish people). He will never abandon the promises he made to King David. He will undoubtedly appoint one of David's descendants to rule over the Jewish people. That's an explicit promise about the Messiah; it's one of the better promises of the new covenant. These are the promises that the writer of the book of Hebrews has in mind when he says the new covenant "is enacted on better promises" (Hebrews 8:6).

BETTER PROMISES FOR THE JEWISH PEOPLE

Now that we have learned a few of the promises of the new covenant, we can see why the Epistle to the Hebrews calls them "better promises." We have not exhausted them all. We could look at more texts from Jeremiah. We could go to the other prophets. We could look at Isaiah, Ezekiel, Amos, Joel, Micah, and so forth, all of whom spoke about the coming Day of the LORD and the final redemption and the kingdom on earth. Isaiah and Ezekiel are packed with promises for the Messianic Era. Those promises are all new-covenant promises because the new covenant is the promise of the Messianic Era. Here's a brief summary of the promises God made to the house of Israel and the house of Judah:

1. I will make a new covenant with them.
2. I will put my Torah within them.
3. I will write my Torah on their hearts.
4. All Israel will know the LORD.
5. I will forgive their wickedness.

6. I will not remember their sins.
7. Israel will never cease to be a nation before me.
8. I will never reject the seed of Israel.
9. I will rebuild Jerusalem as an eternal structure.
10. The entire city will be holy to the LORD.
11. The Messiah will rule on David's throne.
12. The Levitical priesthood will serve in the Temple before me.

The better promises sound great for the Jewish people, but what about the nations? The new covenant prophecy in Jeremiah 31–33 does not mention the other nations at all—at least not in a positive way. They are completely outside of the new covenant, just as they were outside of the old covenant that God made with Israel at Sinai. The other nations are "alienated from the commonwealth of Israel and strangers to the covenants of promise, having no hope and without God in the world" (Ephesians 2:12).

This explains why, prior to the revelation that Peter received in Joppa and the house of Cornelius in Caesarea, the apostles assumed that Gentiles were out of the picture as regards salvation and entrance into the eternal kingdom. This also explains why, prior to the Jerusalem Council, most of the apostles (including Peter) assumed that non-Jewish Yeshua-believers needed to undergo a conversion to become Jewish before they could qualify to enter the kingdom. They were saying, "Unless you are circumcised according to the custom of Moses, you cannot be saved" (Acts 15:1). They were saying, "It is necessary to circumcise them and to order them to keep the Torah of Moses" (Acts 15:5).

It seemed clear according to the better promises of the new covenant. If the Gentile disciples wanted to participate in the better promises of the new covenant, they needed to be part of the house of Israel and the house of Judah. In other words, they needed to be Jewish. "The apostles and the elders were gathered together to consider this matter" (Acts 15:6).

PAUL'S GOOD NEWS FOR GENTILES

Paul taught that Gentile believers did not need to become Jewish to enter the kingdom. He taught that they received an honorary status within the commonwealth of Israel. He taught that they were "grafted in" to the Abrahamic family like a branch grafted onto a tree. He taught that Abraham and the forefathers adopted the Gentile believers as sons and daughters through sharing in the faith of Abraham and the promises given to the Seed of Abraham. He taught that, in the Messiah (the Seed of Abraham), all the families of the earth will be blessed.

The apostles ultimately endorsed Paul's teaching at the Jerusalem Council (Acts 15), and they ruled that Gentile believers did not need to become Jewish to obtain the kingdom. According to the New Testament, Gentile disciples receive a share in the new covenant by virtue of their association with the house of Israel and the house of Judah through the Messiah, the King of the Jews. This is what Yeshua means when he says to the Samaritan woman, "Salvation is from the Jews."

Through the King of the Jews, God graciously extends the benefits of the new covenant to include those peoples living in Israel's conquered territories, so to speak. When Gentile nations surrender to the Jewish King, they become conquered peoples annexed into his kingdom. They become subjects of the kingdom of Judah and, therefore, eligible to benefit from the better promises of the new covenant. Eventually, King Messiah will conquer the whole world and bring all of humanity under the new covenant. Israel will annex all nations because the King of the Jews will conquer us all. Any disciple who has already surrendered to this King is already annexed. The King of the Jews grants his captured Gentiles a type of honorary citizenship under his government along with his people. That's the only reason that I, as a Gentile, have access to the promises of the new covenant. If not for my association with the King of the Jews through submission to him and confession of him as my Master and King, the new covenant would not pertain to me because the new covenant is God's covenant with the Jewish people.

THE NATIONS IN THE KINGDOM

In the Messianic Era, the whole world will fall under subjugation to King Messiah and his government. Then, the whole world will benefit from the better promises of the new covenant. He will place his Torah within the hearts of the Gentiles, as he says, "A law will go out from me, and I will set my justice for a light to the peoples" (Isaiah 51:4). The knowledge of the LORD will extend to all peoples and all nations because all nations will receive revelation through the Spirit poured out on all flesh and through the Torah of Messiah that will go forth from Jerusalem.

The LORD will forgive wickedness and sins and change human hearts. The holy city of Jerusalem will become the capital of the world. The nations will ascend to Jerusalem and the mountain of the LORD, making pilgrimage at the festivals. They will say, "'Come, let us go up to the mountain of the LORD, to the house of the God of Jacob, that he may teach us his ways and that we may walk in his paths.' For out of Zion shall go forth the law, and the word of the LORD from Jerusalem" (Isaiah 2:3).

In the mountain of the LORD and the house of the God of Jacob, the nations will worship the Almighty God of Israel, and his Temple will be called a house of prayer for all nations, as the holy priests, the sons of Aaron, conduct the sacred service. The entire city will be holy to the LORD. Messiah "shall judge between the nations, and shall decide disputes for many peoples; and they shall beat their swords into plowshares, and their spears into pruning hooks; nation shall not lift up sword against nation, neither shall they learn war anymore" (Isaiah 2:4).

All of these better promises lie in the future. Disciples of Yeshua and believers in the risen Messiah have attained a down payment—a deposit on the better promises. We need not wait until the Messianic Era to begin benefiting from the better promises. In Yeshua's name, we identify as citizens of the future kingdom even now and, through him, receive the forgiveness of sins. Through the Spirit poured out on us, we receive a foretaste of the knowledge and revelation of the LORD as the Spirit writes the Torah on our hearts:

> The Son of God, [Yeshua the Messiah], whom we proclaimed among you ... was not Yes and No, but in him it is always Yes. For *all the promises* of God find their Yes in him. That is why it is through him that we utter our Amen to God for his glory. (2 Corinthians 1:19-20, emphasis mine)

CHAPTER FIVE
FROM GLORY TO GLORY

> Behold, the days are coming, declares the LORD, when I will make a new covenant with the house of Israel and the house of Judah, not like the covenant that I made with their fathers on the day when I took them by the hand to bring them out of the land of Egypt, my covenant that they broke, though I was their husband, declares the LORD. (Jeremiah 31:31–32)

The Prophet Jeremiah's prophecy about the new covenant invokes the story of the giving of the Torah at Mount Sinai, the sin of the golden calf, the shattering of the tablets, and the renewal of the covenant through the efforts of Moses. The LORD promises that the new covenant he makes with Judah and Israel will not be like the one made at Sinai, "my covenant that they broke, though I was their husband" (Jeremiah 31:32). That statement alludes to the story of how the children of Israel broke the covenant by making a golden calf (Exodus 32–34). Moses came down Mount Sinai with the tablets of the Ten Commandments. He saw the golden calf and shattered the tablets to signify the broken covenant. For the next forty days, he interceded for Israel in his private Tent of Meeting, beseeching God to forgive the nation. The LORD invited him to come back up the mountain. Moses chiseled out new tablets and went back up the mountain. He spent another forty days on Sinai in God's presence before returning down the mountain with the new tablets. The new tablets symbolized the renewal of the covenant.

THE RENEWED COVENANT AT SINAI

When Moses came down the mountain the second time, his face resplendently reflected the glory of God's presence. In Jewish terminology, the radiance of the Divine Presence is called *Ziv HaShechinah*. The rabbis said, "The radiance of Moses' appearance was like that of the sun and he was like an angel of the Lord of hosts" (*Deuteronomy Rabbah* 11:10).

Moses commanded the people according to all that the LORD had said to him on the mountain. When he had finished speaking, he veiled his face. He removed the veil only when he went into the Tent of Meeting to speak to the LORD. As he emerged to convey the words of the Almighty to the people of Israel, they observed that his face shone. He placed the veil over his face until he went in to speak with the LORD. This implies that the glory on the face of Moses faded over time. The presence of the LORD recharged the luminosity, so to speak, like glow-in-the-dark plastic that needs to be recharged under a light bulb. This chapter takes into account another passage of Pauline material (2 Corinthians 2:17–3:18) to tease out more apostolic theology about the meaning of the new covenant.

A MYSTICAL MIDRASH

> We are not like many, peddling the word of God, but as from sincerity, but as from God, we speak in Messiah in the sight of God. (2 Corinthians 2:17 NASB)

In his second epistle to the Corinthians, the Apostle Paul uses this story to make a mystical midrash that contrasts the difference between the old covenant and the new covenant.

In this part of 2 Corinthians, Paul is on the defensive. Some people in Corinth have challenged his credentials as an apostle. Since he had never personally been a disciple of Yeshua, and since the risen Messiah had not commissioned him during the forty days after the resurrection, his opponents had good grounds for challenging Paul's claim of being an apostle. Paul is defending his ministry and his work.

He points out to the Corinthians that he did not come to them peddling God's Word; that is to say, he did not come to them to make money or raise support from them. He worked with his own hands in Corinth to provide for himself while he taught. He says he and his colleagues are commissioned "as from God, we speak in [Messiah] in the sight of God."

LETTERS OF COMMENDATION

> Are we beginning to commend ourselves again? Or do we need, as some, letters of commendation to you or from you? (2 Corinthians 3:1 NASB)

In those days, the sages sent out letters of approbation along with their apostles. If the sages approved a rabbi or a teacher that they were sending into the Diaspora, they sent him out with a letter of recommendation. The apostles of the sages carried with them credentialing letters. For example, Rabbi Chiya bar Abba sent his apostle to Rabbi Yehudah with a letter that said, "Behold, we send you a great man as our apostle, equal to ourselves until he returns to us" (y.*Chagigah* 76d).

Paul is asking the Corinthians, sarcastically, if they would like a letter of recommendation from the apostles in Jerusalem or from the assembly in Antioch. Or, on the other hand, he asks if he should be carrying a letter of recommendation from the assembly at Corinth. It's a rhetorical question. He answers it himself.

TABLETS OF HUMAN HEARTS

> You are our letter, written in our hearts, known and read by all men; being manifested that you are a letter of Messiah, cared for by us, written not with ink but with the Spirit of the living God, not on tablets of stone but on tablets of human hearts. (2 Corinthians 3:2-3 NASB)

With these words he says that the Corinthian believers themselves are proof of his credentials that he is an apostle of Messiah. He brought Messiah to them, changed their lives, and showed them the way into the kingdom. What more do they need? They are the fruit of his ministry.

Notice how he mixes metaphors, or switches metaphors, I should say. First, he says, "You are a letter from the Messiah, written on our hearts, not with ink, but with the Spirit." Then he switches the metaphor and says that this message of transformation from the Messiah is written "not on tablets of stone but on tablets of human hearts."

This alludes to the stone tablets of the Ten Commandments, the tokens of the old covenant. According to the promises of the new covenant, the Prophet Ezekiel says, "I will remove the heart of stone from their flesh and give them a heart of flesh, that they may walk in my statutes and keep my rules and obey them. And they shall be my people, and I will be their God" (Ezekiel 11:19-20). In similar language, we have heard the prophecy in Jeremiah that says, "I will make a new covenant with the house of Israel and the house of Judah, not like the covenant that I made with their fathers on the day when I took them by the hand to bring them out of the land of Egypt, my covenant that they broke [when they made the golden calf], though I was their husband, declares the LORD. But this is the covenant that I will make with the house of Israel after those days, declares the LORD: I will put my Torah within them, and I will write it on their hearts. And I will be their God, and they shall be my people" (Jeremiah 31:31-33).

Paul takes these two passages, Ezekiel's words about changing our hearts of stone to hearts of flesh, and Jeremiah's words about writing the Torah on our hearts, and he puts them together as he says, "Written not with ink but with the Spirit of the living God, not on tablets of stone but on tablets of human hearts" (2 Corinthians 3:2-4 NASB).

Paul is confident in his credentials through Messiah on the basis of the transformation he has seen in the lives of the believers in Corinth. They are the evidence of his calling.

AMBASSADOR OF THE NEW COVENANT

> Not that we are adequate in ourselves to consider anything as coming from ourselves, but our adequacy is from God, who also made us adequate as servants of a new covenant, not of the letter but of the Spirit; for the letter kills, but the Spirit gives life. (2 Corinthians 3:5-6 NASB)

With these words, Paul claims to be a minister of the new covenant, that is, a teacher of the new covenant. He claims to be an ambassador of the new covenant. He says, "Not of the letter but of the Spirit," which is a contrast addressed in previous chapters. The contrast between the letter and the Spirit refers to the difference between the external

Torah and the Torah written within the heart. Not that they are different standards or different laws, but the Spirit places the supernal Torah within the believer.

The mystics speak about this quite often. They teach that when Messiah comes, he will reveal the Torah of Messiah, just as Moses revealed the Torah at Sinai. The Messiah will reveal the supernal Torah, the inner Torah, from Mount Zion. So the words, "not of the letter but of the Spirit," are just another way of saying, "not of the old covenant but of the new covenant."

What does he mean when he says, "The letter kills but the Spirit gives life"? Paul teaches that the Torah brings condemnation to sinners. The Torah, under the terms of the old covenant, condemns sin. It sentences sinners to death. That's the inflexible standard of God's Torah. Sin begets death. The wages of sin is death. The iniquity of Israel drives the nation into exile.

In the economy of the new covenant, the LORD says, "I will forgive their iniquity, and I will remember their sin no more" (Jeremiah 31:34). The Spirit gives life through the new covenant by changing us.

When compared with the new covenant, the old covenant is a death sentence. For this reason, Paul refers to the embassy of Moses, as he presents the Torah, as "the ministry of death, in letters engraved on stones."

THE MINISTRY OF DEATH

> If the ministry of death, in letters engraved on stones, came with glory, so that of his face, fading as it was, how will the ministry of the Spirit fail to be even more with glory? For if the ministry of condemnation has glory, much more does the ministry of righteousness abound in glory. (2 Corinthians 3:7-9 NASB)

Paul employs the light-to-the-heavy argument, stating that if the covenant at Sinai came with such glory that Moses' face shone, how much more so will the new covenant come with glory. The light on the face of Moses symbolizes the glory of the old covenant. Fading as it was, even so, "the sons of Israel could not look intently at the face of Moses."

For Paul's mystical teaching, the fading glory of Moses' face symbolizes human mortality and this transient created order, which is ever fading: vanity, vanity, a vapor, here today, gone tomorrow. It represents this present world, the material world, which proves ultimately insubstantial. Yet despite that, the revelation of the Torah brought glory into this fading world. It charged the mortal face of Moses with the divine glory of the LORD. Moses reflected the light of immortality in his mortal face.

Moses himself represents the Torah of this world: the Torah of Moses. The supernal Torah, as we know it, has been translated, as it were, into human words, written with ink on physical parchments. It has become incarnate, so to speak, within the world of men as a physical manifestation of the infinite will and wisdom of God. It is divine in origin but physical nonetheless and part of this world. Just as Moses glowed with the glory of God, the Torah has been invested with the light of revelation, the supernal, divine glory of God, but the earthly Torah is still temporal and part of this temporal, fading world.

If the Torah in this present age came with glory, fading though it was, how much more glorious is the brilliant, unfading light of the new covenant of the World to Come.

SURPASSING GLORY

> Indeed what had glory, in this case has no glory because of the glory that surpasses it. (2 Corinthians 3:10 NASB)

Paul says that the glory of the new covenant surpasses that of the old. He says that the glory of the new covenant is so glorious that it makes the old covenant seem like it had no glory at all by comparison. This does not mean that the old had no glory. In fact, if the old had no glory, then it would not take much glory at all to out-glorify it, would it? So, the point is not to disparage the old covenant or the Torah of Moses; the point is to amplify the glory of the new. This is similar to several passages in the book of Hebrews that essentially say, "If you thought the revelation through Moses at Mount Sinai was weighty, how much more so is the revelation through Messiah at Mount Zion?"

THAT WHICH FADES

> If that which fades away was with glory, much more that which remains is in glory. (2 Corinthians 3:11 NASB)

Why does Paul refer to the old covenant as "that which fades away"? Because it is fading away. The old covenant serves as the covenant for this current world. It endures only until the end of this world.

In the Messianic movement, we are fond of quoting the passage where Yeshua says, "Truly, I say to you, until heaven and earth pass away, not an iota, not a dot, will pass from the Law until all is accomplished" (Matthew 5:18). That's true, but notice what happens when heaven and earth do pass away, transformed into a new heaven and a new earth. Does the Torah pass away, too? No. Then the supernal Torah, of which this Torah is only a shadow, will be revealed. The *Midrash Rabbah* says something similar, contrasting the Torah given through Moses and the Torah that will be revealed through Messiah: "The Torah which we study in this world is as nothing when compared to the Torah of Messiah."

The old covenant is fading away along with this world.

As this present world comes closer to the end of the age, winding down, so is the time of the old covenant and the revealed Torah. The writer of the book of Hebrews says, "In speaking of a new covenant, he makes the first one obsolete. And what is becoming obsolete and growing old is ready to vanish away" (Hebrews 8:13). When this world comes to an end, the old covenant will be utterly obsolete, but the new covenant will continue to stand. The old is transitory, but the new covenant is eternal, and the supernal Torah is eternal. The new covenant is the covenant of the kingdom and the World to Come.

BENEATH THE VEIL

> Therefore having such a hope, we use great boldness in our speech, and are not like Moses, who used to put a veil over his face so that the sons of Israel would not look intently at the end of what was fading away. But their minds were hardened; for until this very day at the reading of the old covenant the same veil remains unlifted, because it is removed in Messiah. (2 Corinthians 3:12-14 NASB)

Paul refers here to his countrymen, other Jews in his day, who continued to study the Torah but did not receive the enlightenment of the Inner Torah. This sounds to me much like a Chasid criticizing the *mitnagdim*, those Jews who rejected the teachings of the Chasidim.

The Chasidim speak about the revelation of the concealed Torah that has come through Chasidic teaching, much the same way Paul speaks here about a new revelation of Torah that comes through the Messiah. This is not replacement theology or anti-Judaism. Paul is not talking about Christianity replacing Judaism, Christians replacing Jews, or the gospel replacing the Torah. Instead, he teaches standard Jewish mysticism on this subject. According to Judaism, when Messiah comes, he will reveal the inner dimensions of the Torah. The mystics even call it a new Torah. The Messiah lifts the veil that conceals the inner glory of the Torah. This corresponds to the revelation of which Jeremiah says, "No man will teach his neighbor saying, 'know the LORD,' they will all know me."

SPIRIT OF LIBERTY

> To this day whenever Moses is read, a veil lies over their heart; but whenever a person turns to the Lord, the veil is taken away. Now the Lord is the Spirit, and where the Spirit of the Lord is, there is liberty. (2 Corinthians 3:15-17 NASB)

"Where the Spirit of the Lord is, there is liberty," Paul says. Liberty from what? Liberty from the Law? Liberty from keeping the commandments? Liberty to neglect the letter of the Law? Liberty to sin? No, God gives his Spirit to cause his people to walk in his commandments and statutes, so it makes no sense to think that the Spirit of the LORD liberates us from obedience. Instead, the Spirit liberates us from sin, from condemnation, from punishment, exile, and death.

AS IN A MIRROR

> We all, with unveiled face, beholding as in a mirror the glory of the Lord, are being transformed into the same image from glory to glory, just as from the Lord, the Spirit. (2 Corinthians 3:18 NASB)

The words, "Beholding as in a mirror the glory of the Lord," allude directly to Moses. Numbers 12:6-8 says that the LORD reveals himself to other prophets in visions, dreams, and riddles, but he revealed himself to Moses directly: "If there is a prophet among you, I the LORD make myself known to him in a vision."

In Biblical Hebrew, a vision is called a *mar'ah* (מראה), a word derived from the verb "to see (*ra'ah*, ראה). The word *mar'ah* can also mean "mirror" or "looking glass." For example, Exodus 38:8 speaks of the women donating their mirrors (*mar'ah*, מראה) of polished brass for the laver. When well-polished, the surface of a brass mirror created a reflection, but when tarnished, the reflection in the mirror looked dim and obscured.

Playing on the double meaning of the word—vision and mirror—the *Midrash Rabbah* compares Moses' level of prophecy with that of the other prophets:

> The Rabbis said, "All the other prophets saw their prophetic visions through a tarnished mirror (*mar'ah*), as it is said [in Hosea 12:10], 'I gave numerous visions, and through the prophets I gave parables.' But Moses saw his prophetic vision through a polished mirror (*mar'ah*), as it is said [in Numbers 12:8], 'With him I speak mouth to mouth, clearly, and not in riddles, and he beholds the form of the LORD.'" (*Leviticus Rabbah* 1:14)

This is what Paul alludes to when he says, "Now we see in a mirror dimly, but then face to face" (1 Corinthians 13:12). Moses had a direct line from God. This explains why the words of Moses have higher authority than any other prophet. The words of Moses came directly from God. The mystics say that, in the Messianic Era, we will all attain the level of revelation that Moses experienced:

> In this world the *Shechinah* manifests itself only to chosen individuals. In the world to come, however, [it is written in Isaiah 40:5], "The glory of the LORD will be revealed, and all flesh will see it together; for the mouth of the LORD has spoken." (*Leviticus Rabbah* 1:14)

Paul has the same concept in mind when he says, "We all, with unveiled face, beholding as in a mirror the glory of the Lord, are being transformed into the same image from glory to glory, just as from the Lord, the Spirit."

FROM GLORY TO GLORY

What does the phrase "from glory to glory" mean? It means that we are being transformed from the glory of the old covenant to the glory of the new covenant. It means that we are being transformed from the glory of this present world to the glory of the kingdom and the World to Come. From the glory of the revealed Torah to the glory of the concealed, supernal Torah. From the glory of this physical body to the glory of the resurrected body. From the glory of this mortal, fading world to the glory of the immortal and the divine of the World to Come.

Paul compared the old covenant and the new covenant by making a type of midrash on Moses' glowing face. Paul referred to the "old covenant" as "the ministry of death, in letters engraved on stones" and "the ministry of condemnation" (2 Corinthians 3:7, 9). In contrast to the covenant made at Sinai, Paul referred to the "new covenant" of the Messianic Era (alluding to the prophecies in Ezekiel and Jeremiah) as one "written not with ink but with the Spirit of the living God; not on tablets of stone but on the tablets of human hearts" (2 Corinthians 3:3). He employed the light-to-the-heavy argument, stating that, if the covenant at Sinai came with such glory that Moses' face shone, how much more so does the new covenant come with glory: "For if the ministry of condemnation has glory, much more does the ministry of righteousness abound in glory" (2 Corinthians 3:9).

He compared the veil that covered Moses' face, concealing his glory, to a spiritual veil that obscures the glory of the Torah when it is read by those who have not yet received the revelation of the Messiah.

When we read and study the Torah without the revelation of Messiah, we can be compared to the people of Israel who did not see the glory of the LORD through the veil over Moses' face. The glory lies within the Torah but remains concealed from view. When we read the Torah with faith and in the revelation of Messiah, however, the veil is removed, and we can be compared to one looking directly into the resplendent light of the glory of the LORD because we have entered into a foretaste of the Messianic Era, the kingdom of heaven, already. Then we are transformed "with unveiled face, beholding as in a mirror the glory of the Lord ... transformed into the same image (as Messiah) from glory to glory" (2 Corinthians 3:18).

According to Paul, then, the difference between the old covenant and the new covenant is not the Torah. Both the veiled and the unveiled are reading the same Torah. The difference is that the participant in the new covenant beholds the Torah through the revelation, the unveiling, of Messiah. The participant in the new covenant who sees with eyes unveiled "turns to the Lord" (i.e., repents). The same Torah expresses both the old covenant and the new covenant. The distinction does not arise from a different Torah but from the difference between the people doing the reading.

END OF THIS PRESENT WORLD

By now, it should be clear that a solid interpretation of 2 Corinthians 2:17–3:18 gives us critical tools to understand better the difficult statement in Hebrews 8:13: "In speaking of a new covenant, he makes the first one obsolete. And what is becoming obsolete and growing old is ready to vanish away." The obsolescence of the first covenant pertains not to the obsolescence of God's eternal and unchanging Torah but to the fading away of this present world. As this present world transitions into the Messianic Era and the World to Come, the revelation of the Torah of Messiah written on human hearts surpasses the Torah of Moses as a transformation "from glory to glory." The thing that "is becoming obsolete and growing old" and "is ready to vanish away" is not the Torah but this present world. Heaven and earth will pass away. Death will be swallowed by life. This world is subsumed into the World to Come. The Torah of Messiah will be revealed from within the Torah of Moses. The new covenant will make the old covenant obsolete.

THE SECOND COMING OF MOSES

The story of Moses' first and second trip down the mountain can be compared to the first and second coming of the Messiah. Like Messiah in his first coming, Moses descended to the people with the first set of tablets. "Perhaps I can make atonement for you," Moses told the children of Israel (Exodus 32:30). After his second forty-day fast, he ascended Mount Sinai with the new tablets. There, he remained for another full forty days—a third fast. Back in the presence of God on Mount Sinai, Moses received the great revelation of God's essential person: the Thirteen Attributes. In a similar way, the full extent of God's graciousness, mercy, devotion, and justice became evident only after the Messiah's death and resurrection.

Moses petitioned God for mercy, and God responded, saying, "Behold, I am going to make a covenant." Likewise, the work of Messiah initiated this new covenant.

After forty days, Moses returned to the people with the tablets of the covenant. When he came down among the people, his face shone with the glory of the LORD.

Likewise, when our Master returns, speedily, soon, and in our lifetimes, he will come bearing the new covenant in his arms. He will come in the splendor of his Father's glory, and he will reveal to us the Torah of Messiah, which is concealed in the Torah of Moses.

Until then, our job is to look deeply into the Torah of Moses, seeking the light of the revelation of Messiah, conforming our lives to what we read there, and turning to the LORD so that we might be transformed from glory to glory, as it says, whenever a person turns to the LORD, the veil is taken away.

www.ingramcontent.com/pod-product-compliance
Lightning Source LLC
Chambersburg PA
CBHW052121070526
44586CB00016B/2032